SUCCESS
Secrets
OF
DISRUPTORS

ANTONY ABELL . ANTHONY BASKER .
MARILISE DE VILLIERS . KATE FARAGHER .
DANIEL HAMMOND . RODDY HERBERT .
CHRIS O'HARE . OWEN O'MALLEY .
BARRY PAISLEY . PAULA PETRY . SARAH PIDDINGTON .
ANTHONY POLLOCK . TIM ROBERTSON .
MALCOLM TULLETT . JANE YOUNG . MARK YOUNG

EDITED BY MINDY GIBBINS-KLEIN

a R^ethink Press company

First published in Great Britain in 2022 by
Panoma Press Ltd
www.rethinkpress.com
www.panomapress.com

CONTENTS

FOREWORD

We're all subject to continual disruption in our lives. None of us knows the future, yet the future is coming at an unprecedented pace that we can't keep up with. Futurist Peter Fisk says markets operate four times faster than they did twenty years ago.[1] This warp-speed journey poses the challenge of where to go for support, and it's against this backdrop that we have assembled the disruptors.

Disruptors operate in a world where every industry is being affected by one or all of the following: AI, blockchain, capital markets, climate change, electric vehicles, food shortages, homeworking, inflation, the IoT, robots, scaling cities, the metaverse, water demand and, of course, war. Growth is much harder; companies struggle and leaders worldwide are under immense pressure to pick the right choice. With unlimited options, decision-making becomes close to impossible.

Thirty years of the internet have brought us to a place where we cannot back out, we cannot escape, we cannot choose to avoid facing where we now are. All of us have to operate, and make choices and decisions, in this real-time economy. Where do we turn, and who do we turn to?

---

1   Fisk, P, 'Business Recoded with MAPFRE', Peter Fisk (8 June 2022), www.peterfisk.com/event/business-recoded-with-mapfre accessed 1 July 2022

We turn to the disruptors – individuals who are in the thick of it, living and breathing new world-experiences all day every day. The disruptors are your companions: they walk at your side, they hold your hand, they study the map, they point out different directions and provide insightful choices for you to consider.

I have personally met and spent time with each of the disruptors featured in this book, gaining an understanding of their unique perspective on this unimaginable world we are now entering. By listening to them, you can build up your own patterns, shapes, trends and memes, and apply their skills to the issues you face in your life, in your business, in this universe.

Remember to always take the ORS view: be open, accept random, and be supportive of those around you. Everyone is struggling to keep up and facing their own personal battles. ORS behaviour and thinking allows you to take on board the scale of the shift we are within.

Travel safe. Good luck and if you need anything just ask me @WhatsApp +447875695012.

Thomas Power, co-founder of BIP100

CHAPTER 1

Property... But Not As We Know It

ANTONY ABELL

Property, or real estate, is a fixed asset that we all have a relationship to in one form or another. We all live and work in 'properties' and some of us have worked hard over many years to own them. We may move in and out of them but, almost without exception, properties are permanently 'fixed' by bricks, steel and mortar to wherever they were originally built.

What if all property could be made economically and financially 'liquid', turning what most of us consider an 'illiquid' asset into an instantly transferrable one? What if the value of properties and their title certificates could be easily and safely stored on mobile phones and payment cards, and moved across the world at the speed of light? What if we then discovered that we were able to use liquid property for storing our wealth (and labour) in the form of inflation-resistant 'slices' of legal titles of properties, while that wealth still remained instantly available to us as fiat money to buy goods and services anywhere in the world?

A new form of inflation

A classic definition used by economists for the cause of inflation is 'too much money chasing too few goods'.[2] Our governments (both pre- and post-Covid-19 stimulus payments), banks and trading systems have now created too much money and too much debt and, in equal measure, too much inflation. Too much inflation reduces confidence in the ability of our fiat currencies to hold value or retain their purchasing power. This, and the disrupted supply chains caused by the Covid-19 pandemic, has resulted in the price of goods, energy and services reaching levels never seen before. The CPI (Consumer Price Index) annual inflation rates for May 2022 hit 8.6% in the USA, 9.1% in the UK and a

---

2   Friedman, M, *Money Mischief: Episodes in Monetary History* (Harcourt Publishers Group, 1994)

whopping 222% in Venezuela.[3] The CPI inflation rates in all countries are expected to increase sharply over the next two to fifteen years, coming more and more in line with the much higher monetary inflation rates within each economy. Although not part of the formula used for calculating CPI, the price of property has also continued to increase at rates equal to or greater than inflation.

The advent of new financial technologies, systems and ways of thinking in the property and financial industries is forcing a change in *how* property is used, impacting both access to the asset class and its affordability. The threshold for owning property, who owns it, how it is used and, most importantly, who benefits from it is being globally disrupted. This is the genesis of liquid property.

Aspirational property ownership and the 'miracle' moment

Properties and homes that used to be widely accessible and affordable are no longer so. Many have to wait until their thirties to even hope to be able to buy a home, and delay having families until they can afford one. Traditionally,

3   Trading Economics, 'United States Inflation Rate', (July 2022), https://tradingeconomics.com/united-states/inflation-cpi, accessed 2 August 2022

Gooding, P, 'Consumer Price Inflation, UK: May 2022', Office for National Statistics (22 June 2022), www.ons.gov.uk/economy/inflationandpriceindices/bulletins/consumerpriceinflation/may2022#:~:text=The%20Consumer%20Prices%20Index%20(CPI,of%200.6%25%20in%20May%202021, accessed 2 August 2022

Trading Economics, 'Venezuela Inflation Rate', (July 2022), https://tradingeconomics.com/venezuela/inflation-cpi, accessed 2 August 2022

we would raise a deposit, agree a mortgage or debt for the property, purchase it, and then use it while paying down the debt over time. What most did not know is that the asset-backed financial instruments that were created in this process would then be used by our banks through fractional reserve lending systems to create further digital money for their own benefit, money which would be lent to others to buy *their* own properties. This would be done again and again as our financial systems found that they could create digital money seemingly from nothing, and lend it while charging the recipient of the loan for the privilege.

At the nadir of this process, and prior to the housing crash of 2008/9, the banks in the USA were making 128% of the face value of mortgage documents by using collateralised debt obligations. For fifty years, the process has worked reasonably well in its net effect, creating the excess capital needed to develop new businesses, technologies and growth even while it decreased the purchasing value of fiat money itself. That is until now.

Money printing and the expansion of the money supply over the last fifty-two years, coupled with the accelerated effect of monetary stimulus used in the pandemic, has brought us to the point where our banking systems have arguably created *too* much global debt and *too* much digital money, resulting in unprecedented levels of monetary and consumer inflation. It has also eroded the trust and value previously held in our fiat money and national currencies. This has happened many times before over the millennia – for example, copper was used to debase gold – and it will happen again.

In 1965 an average home in the UK cost £3,353.[4] In 2021 it cost £240,629. Inflation over this period was 1,963% (and 2,051% to July 2022).[5] Owning a home in 1965 cost over four times average earnings and in 2021 the cost was more than nine times average earnings, rising to twelve times average earnings in London in 2022. In a high inflation cycle, property or asset inflation also tends to increase as those with wealth seek inflation-resistant assets, and there is a further increase in the quantity of buyers of the limited supply. This accelerates as the purchasing value of fiat money declines with the increase of inflation. Inflation can be seen in UK house prices which are currently up 12.8% (May 2021 to May 2022) and 18.3% in the USA (May 2021 to May 2022).[6,7] The proportion of average earnings needed to buy a property has continued to accelerate and left property ownership a mere aspiration for many.

4   Love Property, 'UK house prices from the year you were born to today', Love Property (4 November 2021), www.loveproperty.com/gallerylist/55171/uk-house-prices-from-the-year-you-were-born-to-today, accessed 2 August 2022

5   Webster, I, 'The British pound has lost 95% its value since 1965', CPI Inflation Calculator (13 July 2022), www.in2013dollars.com/uk/inflation/1965, accessed 2 August 2022

6   Lewis, C, 'UK House Price Index: May 2022', Office for National Statistics (20 July 2022), www.ons.gov.uk/economy/inflationandpriceindices/bulletins/housepriceindex/may2022, accessed 2 August 2022

7   Trading Economics, 'United States House Price Index YoY', Trading Economics (July 2022), https://tradingeconomics.com/united-states/house-price-index-yoy, accessed 2 August 2022

High inflation is forcing all of us to understand the difference between the real purchasing value of 'money' versus that of fiat 'currency'. It is also forcing us to challenge our understanding of the way that money works for us individually and to ensure that the stored value of our wealth (or our lifetime's work in the form of pensions) may keep ahead of inflation and maintain its future purchasing value. Maintenance of the preserved value of our wealth should include not having to pay a premium to access it. As inflation increases, signs appear that suggest Gresham's monetary law of 'bad money drives out good money'[8] may in fact now be reversing in an asset-based economy where property ownership in a liquid, transparent, secure and transferrable form will increasingly become the preferred unit of exchange as individuals choose for themselves what they will accept in their transactions or as fair value for their labour.

As there is in excess of US$326 trillion of real estate in the world, and the value of it exceeds all other forms of stored or liquid money (both M1 and M2 money supply),[9] the asset-based economy has already started to assert itself as a parallel system to our current fiat/debt economies with their diminishing value and increasing systemic risk. This is seen in the growing number of individuals

---

8   Gordon, J, 'Gresham's Law – Explained', The Business Professor (24 April 2022), https://thebusinessprofessor.com/en_US/economic-analysis-monetary-policy/greshams-law-definition, accessed 2 August 2022

9   Desjardins, J, 'All of the World's Money and Markets in One Visualization', Visual Capitalist (27 May 2020), www.visualcapitalist.com/all-of-the-worlds-money-and-markets-in-one-visualization-2020, accessed 2 August 2022

and institutions using alternative units of exchange in the form of cryptocurrencies and digital assets, whose speed, efficiencies, transparency and low costs undermine traditional legacy banking systems, processes and value propositions. Until the last three years, such an alternative global possibility was not considered viable, as the technologies, regulations, governance, trust structures and efficiencies that were necessary prevented digital representations of real-world assets from being used as money.

These systems are however now ready. The recent rise of blockchain technologies, distributed ledger technologies, AI, regulatory systems and Uniswaps (or automated market maker algorithmic trading systems) have allowed for the seemingly impossible process of turning real-world *illiquid* property into fully *liquid* and transferable money. Without blasphemy or hyperbole, this moment in economic history is as close to a 'miracle moment' in economic history when the world moved to paper specie (fiat currency) or the internet enabled us all to use e-mail.

Half-price homes and going mortgage-free

If properties become fully liquid assets accessible to everyone, our ownership of them and the way that our financial and economic systems operate will irrevocably change. In an asset-based economy with liquid property, ownership of small units of the asset class is affordable for anyone anywhere with a mobile phone, as the cost of owning a fraction of a legal property title drops to 'pennies' with near zero barriers to entry. This is often referred to as the 'democratisation of the ownership of property' and is now very real.

Within the designs of 'sharing economies', liquid property and 'property as money' – the concept that one must use a mortgage product to 'one day' own 100% of a property – is fading. Going 'mortgage-free' no longer needs to be an aspiration, as majority ownership of the title certificates denotes occupancy and control and there is no longer a requirement to fund 100% of the property for these rights. The breakthrough moment is the revelation that the value of owning half of a property is worth far more to our financial and economic systems than it is to the majority owner of the other portion of such a property.

The revolution that is happening in the property industry is that property owners are now starting to ensure that the greater value of their property goes directly to themselves rather than the banks, mortgage providers or intermediaries that previously controlled and gained from the process. As property owners realise the true value of their assets in an open and competitive marketplace, over time they can benefit from their properties by listing, or accessing the stored value of them, on global property exchanges. Making property liquid removes the intermediaries, costs and delays of traditional banking transactions and returns the value of properties directly back to their owners. The true benefit to our societies and our young is that this process enables the creation of 'half-price homes' for those seeking occupancy, equitable equity release for those seeking to go mortgage-free to help fund retirements, equal access to inflation-resistant assets for those seeking to preserve their existing wealth and finally efficient direct access to capital for property developers.

The asset-based economy

Which would you rather be paid for your labours with? A depreciating fiat currency subject to inflation, a highly volatile extrinsic value cryptocurrency or an inflation-resistant unit of intrinsic value liquid property that can then be instantly converted into fiat money at the point of use? In a high-inflation economy, the choice is becoming painfully obvious.

The global delivery of liquid property into an asset-based economy is a unique opportunity to broaden common ownership of the infrastructure of our societies and economies. It promises to combat inflation, reinvent the core principles of capitalism and drive the velocity of money and tax receipts. It is expected to be funded largely by a net inflow of global capital that is currently seeking inflation-resistant assets. In extending the ownership of the essential assets of our economies, liquid property offers the real prospect of rebalancing the unsustainable increase in global wealth disparity and reducing the destruction of the wealth, pensions (stored labour) and savings that inflation inevitably causes in all of our societies.

Antony Abell is the CEO and co-founder of the global TPX™ Property Exchanges in London. A transatlantic serial entrepreneur and global 'break out' technology financier, Antony has worked as an entrepreneur, fund manager and regulated corporate financier in London for twenty-five years.

Antony trained as an economist and political scientist in Canada and the UK and is a former parliamentary researcher, army officer and Winter Olympic coach (1992) who has been directly involved in the creating, funding or running of twenty-three technology companies. His current focus is on the enabling of global digital assets in a new inflation-resistant asset-based economy. He is based in London and on the south coast of England.

🌐 www.tpx-global.com

🌐 https://go.myneproperties.com

🔗 www.linkedin.com/in/antonyabell

CHAPTER 2

The Ubiquity Of Disruption

ANTHONY BASKER

Disruption isn't a 'thing', it's an attitude of mind and iterative process of looking at life through a problem-solving lens to deliver a continuum of improved outcomes. Anybody can be a disruptor – it doesn't require training or a particular skillset. It's an everyday sanity check on the world to see if habits in business or life can be changed for the better.

Am I a disruptor? Sometimes. More often I help deliver disruptive impacts imagined by my clients as the middle and end points of their own disruptive journeys. In my experience, those journeys commonly start with frustration. My typical client is somebody who has become frustrated by inefficiencies in the status quo. This might be because something is too slow, too expensive, too laborious or simply a pain in the butt to achieve. They believe there must be a better way of doing things.

Disruption starts with a perceived problem. It doesn't need to be a widely perceived problem; it's often initiated by an individual. The disruptive journey of communication is the perfect example. It begins when Samuel Morse is frustrated with the speed of postal communication so invents the telegraph and the language that drives it – Morse code – to communicate more quickly at a distance. It continues with Alexander Graham Bell who is frustrated that he cannot speak to people at a distance and invents the telephone. It moves on through the fax machine to Sir Tim Berners-Lee and the World Wide Web.

To be successful, disruption has to have a widely adopted benefit. The technology for the fax machine – the electric printing telegraph – was invented by a man called Alexander Bain in 1843 whom nobody has heard of. It wasn't until Xerox produced the first fax machine in 1964 and sold it into business communities the world over that a successfully disruptive event occurred.

Technology is the servant of disruption

It took five paragraphs to introduce the word 'technology' into this essay. As an aside, I like the word 'essay' in the context of disruption – it comes from the French verb *essayer* meaning 'to try'. Disruptors are all 'essayists', prepared to try and not afraid to fail.

For many people, technology is disruptive in its own right. I have a different perspective. For the most part I see technology as the servant of disruption, a means of delivery developed in response to resolving a frustration. Another way of looking at it would be that technology is the partner of disruption. When you consider the fountain of disruption that is Apple, it seems evident that the devices they produce, while beautifully designed and engineered, are developed as servants of society.

Here's a question: who was the disruptor at Apple? Was it Steve Wozniak, who created the technology, or Steve Jobs who saw the 'vision of better'? Given that Steve Wozniak had to disrupt established technologies and design to deliver the vision in a layout and at a price the world thought offered good value, I guess they both were; but the vision came first.

In the context of technology, which is the space within which I work, it is interesting to consider the yin and yang of disruption – software and hardware. A great example is the way people enjoy music. The earliest tech disruptions were in the hardware, from cylinder to disc, to tape, to personal cassette. All of these were analogue devices designed by engineers. As such, design itself can be disruptive.

Then the digital age started in 1991 when the wonderfully named Karlheinz Brandenburg, wanting to compress Suzanne Vega's song 'Tom's Diner' into as small a space as he could without affecting the sound, created the MP3 file.

The first MP3 player got no market traction. It wasn't until the release of the iPod in 2001 that the software and hardware came together and were widely adopted, and a change which disrupted the market occurred. Sometimes, successful disruption has to wait for the right time and the right place.

I fully admit that while I would claim to have the engineer's mindset of solving problems and making life better, my focus is the way that software can run on existing protocols within a digital environment.

Disrupting to order

As mentioned above, I work in a world where I mostly respond to clients' requests. I disrupt to a brief. I think that's an interesting viewpoint. Due to issues of confidentiality (I've lost count of the number of NDAs I sign every year) I can't name specific clients or projects, but I've worked for some of the biggest brands in Europe and a raft of smaller companies. Just about all have approached me with a 'Wouldn't it be nice if…' sort of brief.

Many of the smaller companies have been start-ups whose entire *raison d'être* and business plan is based on disruption. Mostly their proposition is 'Wouldn't it be nice if we could do XYZ... and make a fortune.' I have no objections to capitalism!

Other, bigger organisations approach me from a customer service proposition. I've worked extensively with the pharmaceutical and healthcare sector where the motivation for disrupting the system is 'Wouldn't it be nice if we could diagnose this condition earlier or make treatment delivery more effective.' These projects are usually delivered as a free value-add and enhance the brand or service reputation – they also genuinely save lives.

It may be a truism but, for disruption to be successful, disruptors need to know what success looks like. Is it improving outcomes or is it making money? In many cases, the key to successful disruption is a blended option of both.

In the early days of video streaming, Netflix, needing investment, approached the Blockbuster Video rental network and offered itself for sale. Blockbuster, perhaps because they had thousands of videos in stock, a stable overhead and a tried-and-tested process, turned them down. They failed to appreciate how the digital world was revolutionising the world of on-demand entertainment. Many of us will remember walking through a cold, dark winter's night to the video store only to find somebody had already taken out the film we wanted.

Blockbuster Video opened its doors in 1985. At its peak in 2004, it owned over 9,000 stores and employed 85,000 people. In a similar fashion, Netflix actually started as a rent-by-mail video service in California in 1997 but, by 2007, had morphed its business model to a streaming service that film fans flocked to in their millions – as recently as 2020 Netflix had over 150 million members and Netflix streaming accounted for 15% of all internet bandwidth.

With a wide range of films and television programmes, Netflix's subscription service completely disrupted the video store pay-by-title business model. In 2010 Blockbuster, having failed to understand 'what success looked like' filed for Section 11 bankruptcy with debts of US$900 million.[10]

Today Netflix itself is under pressure from challenger brands such as Apple TV, Amazon and Disney. They may not disrupt the market in the way Netflix did, but they have every chance of disrupting Netflix.

The role of repetition

There is always more than one way to solve a problem. On one hand, national governments are desperately trying to solve the climate change problem – disruption

---

10   Sloan, M, 'Netflix Vs Blockbuster – 3 Key Takeaways', Drift (1 June 2020), www.drift.com/blog/netflix-vs-blockbuster, accessed 15 July 2022

writ in neon capital letters − by legislating against the amount that can be produced. On the other hand, engineers are beavering away industriously trying to find ways to eliminate the problem from the production cycle. In many ways, this is two sides of the same coin, but it is two completely different mindsets: one saying 'ban it', the other saying 'let's manage it'.

How disruptive is disruptive? How big a change do you need to make to something to deliver a big difference?

The starting point for any of my involvements in problem-solving is scoping. First scope the size of the problem. Then scope the range of possible solutions. Then decide the direction of the approach. It's important to stress here the value of experience. While many client businesses are seeing their problem for the first time, I could well have solved similar problems, in principle, multiple times. I know what works.

Having said that, every brief is different and every solution is an enhancement of the one before. The fact is that every scoping exercise is disruptive in its own right. Technology evolves at an exponential rate, so delivering disruptive solutions becomes a layer-upon-layer process. While in every way my team are professional deliverers of disruption, they are on a continuous learning curve. Every scoping exercise opens new opportunities − we make sure to keep on top of tech developments and new protocols.

Disruption without efficiency is anarchy

In my world, delivering disruption always results in improved efficiency. Disruption for disruption's sake is simply anarchy. Whatever the next iteration might be, it has to deliver better efficiency and value than its predecessor. There is always a requirement for a customer value-add whether that is a better price, better speed, better reporting or simply a more comfortable user journey.

This brings me back to the point that any disruption is only successful if it's followed by mass adoption. Uber has perhaps been one of the most disruptive companies in the history of disruption, taking on the vested interests of transport establishment across some of the world's largest cities. It has fought some major regulatory battles and, rightly, had to completely renegotiate its stance on employees.

Many businesses, faced with such struggles, might have packed up and gone home. Not Uber. It has continually rolled with the punches based on the belief that over 120 million active monthly users worldwide want a hailing service they can not only run from their phone but which saves them money.

The Uber model meets my disruptive criteria of value-add and efficiency. Today, well in excess of 3 million people drive for Uber and it fulfils over 20 million rides per day.

Budgeting to disrupt

Many people think disruption is expensive. It doesn't need to be. A buddy of mine is a dyslexic author on a mission to democratise reading for dyslexics and the neurodiverse. He wanted his new novel to have a 'dyslexia-friendly' iteration.

Like most authors, he had no budget – but he didn't need one. He had known for some time about a specific typeface called OpenDyslexic, designed to help those who struggle to read. Then he saw some research in the newspaper about an academic project that proved increasing the spacing between words and lines made books more accessible.

He called the university in question who were delighted to help, spoke to his publisher and had the book formatted and typeset a different way. Leveraging Amazon print-on-demand technology, the special 'dyslexia-friendly' edition has gone live. All it cost was time and inspiration and he is hoping that others will follow suit, which will completely disrupt the publishing process.

Oncosts and disruption in practice

There is an oncost to disruption. There are winners and losers. Blockbuster and the entire VHS industry went out of business. Regular taxi services lose revenue to Uber. Hotels lose revenue to Airbnb. At the same time, the world benefits – but this is the nature of business and, in particular, the nature of technology.

Delivering successful disruption is my day job, but I don't see myself as an innovator of disruption. Rather, I'm good at my job and know how to do it. From my perspective, anybody can be a disruptor – all you need is the vision of changing something for the better. You might need some help to get there, but the important thing is the volition and determination to make a change.

Anthony Basker grew up as a grassroots techie, journeying through hardware and peripherals, operating systems and software to websites and apps. He has a 360 degree helicopter view of how technology facilitates communication and delivery.

People knew Anthony was an uber-geek when he started mapping the shortest distances on his pizza delivery route – years before the thought crossed Google's mind. He has been solving problems ever since.

'Technology,' he says, 'should only ever be the servant of a good idea.' He has used this philosophy to grow ideas from zero into multimillion-pound businesses. Along the way he has developed the ability to provide the consistent and inspirational leadership required to build, guide and engage multidisciplinary teams.

In 2020 Anthony was named innovator of the year by Provoke Media.

🌐 www.anthonybasker.com

in www.linkedin.com/in/anthonybasker

CHAPTER 3

Wake Up! Master Your Six Higher Mental Faculties

MARILISE DE VILLIERS BASSON

Living on autopilot is the opposite of being mindful. You let your brain's automatic function kick in for daily habits, thought processes and decisions. You do things without thinking, you overcommit, you forget parts of your day, you waste time, you feel like you're existing rather than living. You miss chances to learn and grow.

Unfortunately, this is true for many people. Earl Nightingale said, 'Most people tiptoe their way through life hoping they make it safely to death.' A study was done on 100 elderly hospital patients, who were asked to reflect on their life's biggest regret. Nearly all of them said it wasn't the things they did, but the things they didn't do – the risks they never took, the dreams they didn't pursue. They never realised their dreams because they allowed self-doubt and outside circumstances to overpower and crush them.

My life's work is centred around helping people to find their ROAR! – to live their best life: with **purpose**, in their **power** and with the **courage** to speak their truth. ROAR is also a four-step process for having courageous conversations – with yourself and others. It stands for **Recognise**, **Observe**, **Assert** and **Redirect**.

Notice the conversation you're having with yourself. Are you committed to your freedom, or are you committed to suffering? Do you have a positive, can-do attitude or are you allowing outside circumstances and self-doubt to get in the way of your dream? Are you saying to yourself: 'I don't know how', 'I don't have the time or money', 'What if I try and they don't like it?', 'I've tried before and it didn't work', 'I'll try it when…'?

You have a power flowing through you that, if you harness and cultivate, can make all your dreams come true. You must win your inner game with your thoughts and feelings, and win your outer game with your words and actions. You can turn any limiting conversation into a powerful ROAR.

- **Recognise** what is happening inside you right now. What limiting thoughts and feelings are coming up for you? Name it. When you name a fear, it loses its power.

- **Observe** and allow yourself these thoughts and feelings. Don't try to get rid of them, or ignore them, or fix them. Stay present.

- **Assert** by having an honest conversation with yourself. Respectfully acknowledge that whatever is coming up for you is the reality of the moment. Simply ask: 'Is it true?'

- **Redirect** your thoughts and feelings and recalibrate the conversation by turning it into empowering one, aligned with your higher self.

If you're not happy with your current results, it's time to disrupt your mind. It's time to turn your thoughts, feelings, words and actions into superpowers. It truly is an inside job. Opt today for your dream, for your freedom. Commit.

Shifting gears

When I say: 'You have all the power inside you to make all your dreams come true', notice what you're thinking and how you're feeling. Don't judge yourself, just notice what you're noticing. If you think you can do something, you'll find a way, no matter what. If you think you can't, that mindset is going to stop you, cripple you and you will move into a life of complaining and believing that it's just never going to work out for you. Henry Ford summed this up eloquently when he said, 'Whether you believe you can do a thing or not, you are right.'

I am here to tell you that you have an extraordinary mind, with six higher mental faculties, your superpowers – imagination, intuition, will, memory, reason and perception.

We think in pictures, but we don't know what our minds look like. Have you ever thought about creating a picture of your mind? The brain and the mind are not the same thing. Our brain is a physical organ associated with our body, whereas the mind refers to our mental programme, our thought processes.

Consider this: you live simultaneously on three planes:

1. You are a spiritual being.

2. You have a miraculous mind.

3. You live in a physical body.

Your thought energy lies in the spiritual, nonphysical world. You've been gifted an intellect, and by using your six higher mental faculties you can tap into this thought world to dream big and build ideas.

The stick figure

Around 1934, Dr Thurman Fleet, a chiropractic healer and teacher of metaphysics, created an image to show patients how they could heal their bodies by controlling the mind.[11] It's called 'the stick figure'. Imagine a simple stick person with a large circle representing the head, and a smaller circle underneath representing the body.

Now take the large circle and divide it in half. The top half is the conscious mind, the thinking mind (**thoughts**). The bottom half is the subconscious mind, the emotional mind (**feelings**).

Let's start with the conscious mind. This is where your free will lies, in those six mental faculties that enable you to choose your thoughts, accept or reject any idea. No person or circumstance can cause you to think about ideas that you do not choose. Imagine a funnel of energy going right into the crown of your head. This energy flowing into your consciousness has no form. It's neither positive nor negative. It just is. You can build any picture you want. This is important because the thoughts you choose will eventually determine your results in life. Take a moment and ask yourself: what do I want? Or better still: what would I love? I want you to visualise yourself with the good you desire. Create a picture in your mind. Now let's turn that picture over into your subconscious mind.

---

11   Proctor, B, *You Were Born Rich* (LifeSuccess Productions, 16 January 1997)

Visualise seeing that beautiful picture drifting down through an imaginary psychic barrier into the subconscious mind. Every **thought** or **word** your conscious mind chooses to accept must also be accepted by the subconscious mind, which is in every cell of your body and has no ability to reject the picture you show it. Your subconscious operates in an orderly manner by law, bathing the image it receives in emotion. Those emotions control the vibration that your body is in and must move the body into **action**. When you hear someone say 'I feel good' or 'I feel bad', what they are really saying is: 'I am consciously aware of the vibration I am in.' The thoughts and pictures that you consciously choose and impress upon your subconscious mind control your vibration. Your vibration controls your actions. The actions you take or don't take determine your **results**.

The moral of the story? Any thought – good or bad – that you repeatedly impress upon your subconscious mind becomes fixed. Fixed ideas, more commonly known as habits, will then continue to express themselves automatically, on autopilot, until they are replaced. To change your results, you are going to have to change your thoughts, feelings, words and actions. It's that simple.

Are you ready to master your six higher mental faculties?

Your superpowers

To create and manifest the life you've always wanted, instead of just getting by day-by-day on autopilot in a life you're simply settling for, you must learn to harness and master your six higher mental faculties. You are using them already, whether you know it or not, you're just likely not utilising them to the maximum capacity. I use my four-step inner **ROAR** process to check in with myself and recalibrate whenever I catch myself engaging in negative self-talk. It's like a muscle that needs exercising and growing constantly.

Let's dive deeper into the six higher mental faculties.

1. **Imagination** is the most fabulous tool we've been given, and probably the one you're most familiar with. It allows you to dream big and imagine a life you truly want, like you did earlier. You may not be aware yet of how you're utilising it and whether it is working for you or against you. Most of us, including myself sometimes, use imagination to our detriment; we use it to terrorise ourselves, to create the crazy circumstances that we don't want to happen. You are meant to use your imagination to create whatever you desire, to design a life that you love.

2. **Intuition** is often called our sixth sense, a deep knowing. There have probably been times in your life when you made decisions despite a niggling feeling that it wasn't the right decision for you. I have, many times, when I didn't follow my intuition, my gut, that small still voice inside.

Intuition is your nonlinear intelligence system, your higher self. You're an infinite being having a human experience. Intuition is that marvellous mental faculty that gives us the conscious ability to pick up vibration, pick up another person's thoughts, read their energy.

3. **Will** is powerful. It gives us the ability to hold one idea in our consciousness without any distractions. Many of us know willpower. That's not what we're talking about here. Will is not force. It's the ability to hold one idea on the screen of your mind to the exclusion of all outside distractions that are begging for your attention through your five senses. When someone asked Dr Wernher von Braun what it would take to put a man on the moon, von Braun replied simply: 'The will to do it.' That's it. Everything else is tactics, you can figure it out. You must have the will to do it. To harness your will, focus your attention on that which you desire.

4. **Memory** can never be bad. Everyone has a perfect memory. You can develop your memory to a phenomenal degree. Most people believe they have weak memories when they can't remember things. This isn't true; we all have a perfect memory. There is so much still to learn about the science. Some studies have shown that when people are hypnotised they can perfectly recall every moment of their life, even the moment

they were born. When you look at neuroscience, the same area that lights up in your brain when you're remembering something in the past, lights up when you imagine something in the future – so, in that moment of imagining, you are 'remembering' your future. I know, right? It's mind-blowing.

5. **Reason** in this context is right reason, not common-sense reasoning. Most people use their five senses to reason away their success. Right reason is higher faculty (or inductive) reasoning. You went through this thinking process earlier with the stick figure when you created a picture in your mind of the good you desire. Thinking is the highest function that you're capable of.

6. **Perception** is how we see things. Perception is reality. We use perception all the time, and most often to terrorise ourselves. Your perception is the meaning that you give to something. We must learn to harness and cultivate our perception so that we can create and attach meaning that aligns with our dreams. We don't deny our circumstances, consequences or situations, but we deny the power they have over us. As Wayne Dyer famously said: 'If you change the way you look at things, the things you look at change.'[12]

12   Dyer, Dr, WR, 'Success Secrets', www.drwaynedyer.com/blog/success-secrets, accessed 6 July 2022

When we use our six higher mental faculties – our superpowers – we bring whatever we desire into creation. We must learn how to activate, harness, cultivate and use the six mental faculties for the gifts that they are for us. Are you ready to get into the driving seat of your mind and have courageous conversations with yourself?

Wake up! Dream big. Get out of your own way. Make your best life a reality. Don't die with your ROAR! still inside you.

Marilise de Villiers Basson is a certified high-performance coach, bestselling author, TEDx speaker and award-winning behaviour change consultant who specialises in cybersecurity awareness, culture and talent. She's a podcast host, international keynote speaker and regular podcast guest. Passionate about helping people live successful, healthy and free lives, Marilise is the founder and CEO of ROAR!

Marilise's approach combines over two decades of experience as a chartered accountant, coach and change consultant. She encourages organisations to move away from compliance-led, tick-box approaches towards a working environment that embeds cyber safe mindsets and habits through risk-based, people-centric methods. She emphasises the need for a speak-up culture that allows suspicious behaviour and mistakes to be surfaced and addressed.

🌐 www.marilise-de-villiers.com

 www.linkedin.com/in/marilise-de-villiers-9184521a

CHAPTER 4

Successful Horizon Meetings

KATE FARAGHER

Meetings are often boring, long and ineffective, with the main outcome to have another meeting. In times of systemic change, we need solutions to complex problems. How do you make decisions in turbulent times? The answer is that we need to improve meetings. This chapter is not about meetings that share information. This is about horizon meetings: meetings that require decisions to be made about problems on the horizon.

I have observed hundreds of meetings of parliamentarians, senior leaders and middle management. Often, the most highly paid and busiest people sit and say little to quicken the meeting's end. There is an apathy towards interjecting because participants have not had time to understand the problem and they'd rather stay silent than sound ignorant. At the other end of the scale, there are people who fight to talk and air their opinions, competing to get noticed. Neither of these situations makes for good decisions or outcomes.

In the majority of cases, those who speak the most have primed the other attendees, hold the most senior positions or are from the most feared department, and often determine the outcome. Decisions are frequently made by a minority of people. This is meeting bias. I've seen and heard of crazy decisions that have had detrimental impacts on societies and businesses being made in this way.

Complex problems require a well-designed space to think. How do we get into the right headspace to make agile and bold decisions in meetings? How can we stop ourselves from deciding the outcome of the meeting before we enter the room? How can we stop believing that we are right, when our only perspective is from the high ground? The secret ingredient to great meetings is to be confused and conflicted.

Confused

I have worked in the parliamentary sector for over fifteen years and have learned that when you want to change things you need to have resolve, resilience and a refusal to take no for an answer. The parliamentary sector is where the power MPs wield soft power. Hard power is reserved for government ministers who can implement the action. Soft power can be used to help those with hard power to think better.

Horizon meetings improve the quality of decisions, the quality of scrutiny and can identify the direction of travel. Sometimes, that will mean stopping something that isn't working. In my experience, this is a huge mindset challenge. Many don't want to lose face so pursue bad ideas. Better meetings will stop bad decisions and find better, braver solutions.

A good horizon meeting needs to feel messy and uncomfortable. If you allow the discomfort, you allow new ideas to emerge. When a new problem arises, it's not always easy to articulate the complexity of the response needed. Often it's an instinct, a part of an answer. Here are a few pointers for how you might approach this.

1. Feel weird

To solve problems, you need a united vision but you don't need united values. Differences stretch our thinking. This can mean people will feel triggered, angry and annoyed.

If they're still listening, they will feel confused. Part of feeling confused is losing the thread and feeling out of control. Go with this. Clarity lives at the other end. Keep listening through the weirdness. A good facilitator can help; even better, teach your leaders the art of facilitating these types of meetings.

2. Trust the weirdness

When we feel confused and out of control, we do everything to try to keep the status quo. Our judgement kicks in; we disagree. We get annoyed by what we perceive to be others' stupidity. Our ego gets louder: we are right and they are wrong. We shake our head and can't see the logic in their argument. We make assumptions; we voice our preconceived ideas; we interrupt their flow and stop listening to anything that disagrees with our point of view.

What happens if we do the opposite? We trust the weirdness and disrupt the status quo. We learn to give others in the meeting the space to feel and be weird. To explore their thoughts even when they don't seem logical. We stop our judgement, believe there are no wrong or right thoughts. We suspend logic and assumption and try to listen beyond it. We notice the anger and discomfort, but see this as information to keep listening, not judge.

In select committees in parliament, MPs holding different beliefs come together to scrutinise government officials.

It works when there is respect. In well-run committees I often hear, 'We might disagree with... however...' If you respect the person with a different point of view from yours, you can use that difference to stretch your thinking.

3. Think together

If you can feel and trust the weirdness you can start to think together. Thinking together is a communication technique that requires you to step into the unknown. This blind spot is often where the answers to the most difficult problems lie. Only with confusion can we find the key to that quadrant. In social media, on TV programmes, in the news and in education we are consistently taught that debate, opinion and influencing are the keys to unlocking solutions. We need to feel confused before we learn. It's how our neurons rewire.

I would imagine some of you may be thinking, 'This is ridiculous, how can this solve problems?', 'We need clear strong leadership, not namby-pamby BS,' or 'It's critical thinking, logical argument and debate that helps solve problems, not giving up our expert opinion.' To think together we need to disagree together, which is why conflict is an essential part of great meetings, better decision-making and deeper learning. Let's clarify what thinking together is and isn't.

Co-create

Brainstorming is recalling information. Brainstorming can involve ego. It is where you want to say something that makes you look good. It can also be that you use language you've used before, stories you've told before and ideas you've heard before. It is a great way to share information.

Thinking together is not brainstorming. When you think together you co-create.

Thinking together requires a shift in mindset and brain use. It's where you listen and respond to an idea in real time. It requires you to say something you don't completely understand yet. It's messy. On one level it's simple – be idea-led. On another level it's complex – don't follow the certainty.

To do this you have to hold the new idea and integrate your thoughts. You offer part of an idea to evoke the other's response, then start building the idea together. You hear what they say and make an offer: 'That makes me think…' If you feel disagreement, put it aside. This part of thinking together is about saying yes and suspending judgement.

You need to get rid of certainty and assumption to open up the spatial part of your brain. It can feel weird. A bit like brain yoga. You are stretching your thinking to take into account other ideas that you might disagree with.

This spatial brain use helps us move through physical places and it also helps us navigate ideas.

You need to feel safe to do this kind of thinking. You need to know you won't lose your job, your position or your status if you say something silly or controversial. You need to say what comes to mind even if it goes against the current narrative. The more people bravely say the unsaid, the richer the quality of the discussion and the better the decisions made further down the line. You need to create these spaces to rise to the challenge of these types of meetings. You know the meetings are working when the confusion leads to courageously disagreeing and allowing positive conflict.

Conflicted

Positive conflict requires trust. You need to be comfortable with people disagreeing with you. As I said previously, this needs to be supported with mutual respect.

Positive conflict requires everyone to be able to voice their discomfort. You need to be able to say, 'This is making me feel angry.' Anger can be a useful emotion as long as it doesn't turn into aggression. If you get to that point, work out the best solution. It might be that everyone needs to take a break, or people are allowed to leave and return without the rest of the attendees trying to rescue the person.

Inner conflict is a great teacher. It means we're growing and there might be a new approach emerging.

Here are three ways to facilitate conflict in meetings:

1. Set out some guidelines to help people know how to communicate during conflict

The aim here is to pre-empt what could go wrong so if it does there's a strategy already in place to deal with it. It helps avoid confusion. You simply refer to what was previously agreed. Ask people to speak with respect and to use 'I' statements so they take ownership of the topic.

The goal is to create a safe space for people to voice opposing thoughts without the fear of being shut down or ridiculed. I find that when these thoughts can be fully heard there are places of overlap. You need to allow these to emerge. It's important to realise that conflict comes in many forms: inner, outer and cultural. Guidelines help navigate them.

2. Use visual prompts

To activate the spatial problem-solving brain, create visuals. Use timelines to record ideas, holding boards for those ideas that don't quite fit yet, theme boards to explore multiple issues at the same time. These visual prompts can be either online or in person.

3. Ask people to build on ideas rather than state opinions

Rather than saying 'I think', use 'That makes me think…' Solving together ideally comes from that unknown unknown place. It starts from an instinct of knowing without being able to form the words around it.

If you are experienced in your role, your instinct has hidden wisdom. If your meeting includes people who live the problems daily, these instincts are rich in understanding. When you think and solve together, new narratives are created, not reworded.

Review

There is a fourth 'r' that is required in this process. After resolve, resilience and refusal to take no for an answer comes review.

Coaches and trainers often feel the need to end sessions with actions, but when you think together in disruptive/ horizon meetings you often need a time of reflection. You need to move into the slow brain. This percolation time is important. It's like we're running the thoughts through our experience. We see what remains, what pops up and what emerges. Ideally, you want to sleep on it because that's when your unconscious makes sense of the unknown unknown.

It's important to know when to stop a meeting. Meetings get too long if you allow people to talk about their opinions rather than co-create. If you plan the visuals well and if the group have embedded trust, it's incredible how quickly you can disrupt. Humans work well with deadlines. A bit of healthy stress can help you think deeply.

It is possible to find clarity from complexity. We just need to disrupt our ego. The secret ingredient is navigating our confusion, feeling comfortable with conflict and facilitating braver, better solutions by thinking together. Go forth and disrupt. How we meet matters.

Kate Faragher has been a communication consultant for nearly twenty-five years. She has worked in the corporate sector, training people to write, speak, question and influence without bias. She creates bespoke awaydays and horizon scanning sessions for parliamentarians, academics and C-suite executives. Her unique methodology uses a variety of techniques to help people learn quickly, listen deeply and collaborate across political, cultural and ideological divides. Her passion is creating safe collaborative spaces for meaningful change.

Prior to her consultancy, she worked in BBC news, TV sales and distribution, theatre and film production and performance. She has performed at the National Theatre, on the TEDx stage about intuitive collaboration and has her own podcast, *Listen to the Whisper.*

CHAPTER 5

Let's Get Uncomfortable

DANIEL HAMMOND

I try not to get too comfortable, because comfort equates to stagnation. I earn a living by disrupting my clients' businesses and organisations in ways that reveal risk and opportunity and create transformation, and by making sure they have the support they need to be significantly better off on the other side of the disruption.

I have worn a few hats, and I bring my lifetime toolbox with me on every opportunity to serve my clients. For every role, I have tackled the most difficult problems, learned new skills to proficiency, and served people to the best of my abilities. Without any effort (aka conniving or politicking) beyond employing this strategy, so far I have been blessed to work with Cabinet-level leaders in four countries, in four different job roles. I refuse to let myself get too comfortable and I encourage you to do the same by thinking about what you want to achieve and asking yourself questions around what you are doing to get there.

Imagine your amazing life

How have you explored what makes you uncomfortable to find hidden opportunity, risk and growth? We all seek some level of certainty and clarity. What opportunities are you looking for to improve your life? Nigerian princes who want to give you millions are too good to be true, but how often do we let a genuine opportunity pass by because we are comfortable with what we know? Burying your head in the sand to be able to say 'I see no danger here' leaves you woefully unprepared when a hungry pack of wolves comes along.

What do you want your future to look like? If you want to grow your life over time, you need to be actively seeking the training, education, skills and new perspectives that will allow you to move in that direction. Are you living your absolute best life, whatever that means for you? Do you have a list of five places in your life that could benefit from some sort of improvement, or could you create one? Let's explore what an over-the-top amazing life might look like.

You own one or more successful businesses, but they don't own you. You are making multimillions of dollars per year. You spend your time at work doing what you love to do, and you never work longer than you want to. Your companies manage themselves and your employees love coming to work and serving your clients. You are married to the person of your dreams and you love spending time together, travelling where you love to go and doing what you love to do. Together you are raising the ideal number of children (or pets, or plants) that you desire, and they are exceptional, and amazingly well behaved. You are highly respected in your business field(s) and in all of your local communities. You own several homes and split your time between them. You can invest as much time and money as you like in your hobbies and non-profit causes. You have had some tough times in your life, but you learned from them and they added to your success and your ability to help and connect with others. Everyone who knows you likes, respects and trusts you. Where you want to be influential you are having a positive transformational impact in the lives of others. Your future, the futures of your family and of your businesses are as guaranteed as any future ever is.

How close did that description match up to your current life? Is it where you are currently headed? Where did it fall short of what you have already achieved? Not everyone wants to own businesses, and of course it is perfectly fine if you are not someone who does, but if not, are you working in your dream job, with a dream boss, building something that makes a big difference in the world where your time and commitment are rewarded with enough money to provide abundantly, and enough time off to enjoy it? We will come back to this example later; for now, let's look at some of the key components of this 'good' life when it comes to making a 'good' living.

Your work-life goals

Do you love going to work? If every week you wake up thinking, 'Thank goodness it's Monday!' and that isn't your normal day off, you are probably doing what you love to do. You are likely putting your unique skills, experience and giftedness towards creating something or solving something that is transforming lives. If you are excited to do what you do, you are working from your uniqueness.

A big reason we work is to pay our bills. How well compensated are you for what you do? Maybe you were born to be a graffiti artist. If so, hopefully you get well paid to decorate the sides of buildings. You also have the option to do a job that is not a good fit but pays for a hobby, a passion, a calling; or to pursue the side hustle that will someday become a real business that will pay all the bills, and then some. Maybe you have found a niche where you are paid a ridiculous amount of money to do next to nothing.

A third component to work is whether you are valued and appreciated. Many of my peers are entrepreneurs and some of them still don't like who they work for. Just because you own a business doesn't mean you are your own boss – the clients that keep you in business need to be taken care of, or you won't have a business. The best boss I ever had was my wife, but sometimes that left me inside 120-degree Fahrenheit shipping containers loading heavy boxes and taking inventory.

Envision your future

Beyond the work side of living, what else do you want? Do you want to have a family, to travel, to make a difference with a non-profit, etc? Where do you want to live? What kind of people do you want to spend time with? How do you want to be remembered? What else matters to you?

Before I suggest some ideas for how you might disrupt yourself, I want to pose two more questions. They both refer back to my example of what I thought was a pretty 'good', although quite generic, life. Number one: while it might have felt like a lifetime of hard work and amazing accomplishments, if you had achieved all of those things by the age of twenty-five, what would you do with the rest of your life? Number two: what if, like me, you have plans big enough that that level of success is not sufficient? Wealth can eventually grow itself, but people grow when they do something new and uncomfortable.

Once you stop growing, you start to die, and most of us get to decide when that is.

Here are some of the areas where I allowed myself to become uncomfortable in my life. I hope they will give you some ideas of how you might grow in some useful way.

At age eight, I went to a summer camp without any of my friends; it was a very uncomfortable time. At fifteen, I worked on a farm in a foreign country for several months. At twenty, I left a job I had mastered to gamble on my ability to grow faster somewhere else. At twenty-three, I signed a four-year military enlistment contract, committing me to learning a foreign language and jumping out of airplanes. I volunteered for new things in the military and got 'voluntold' for others, such as exploring what Special Forces training could do for my career (and then decided not to pursue it because it wouldn't get me where I wanted to go – getting uncomfortable isn't only about saying 'Yes').

I left the active Army when it no longer aligned with my goals; I had had enough discomfort being away from my baby boy. I joined the Reserves, changed jobs, became an instructor, and looked for short-term job opportunities in foreign lands (Panama and Hawaii). I learned how to SCUBA dive. I volunteered for a mission trip to Honduras to build houses (inspired by my sister's service there), and while there I jumped off a cliff into a river without knowing how high the cliff was (it was 22 meters/72 feet) or how deep the river was (although I had seen others jump and dive off it).

Even when forces outside my life blew-up my plans, I looked for opportunities to learn, grow and serve. For example, when I was demoted, transferred to a unit where I didn't know anyone and was deployed for fifteen months (mostly in a war zone), the first thing I started doing was volunteering for every not fun job, including volunteering to clean fifty-year-old bathrooms in bad shape. Why? Because by becoming an asset to leadership as early as possible, my options and opportunities expanded over the period that I was going to serve with them.

An action plan for disruption

If you are young, look at one area of your life that you want to improve and invest in your growth; then, as you get where you want to be, find a new area. Spend less than you make as often as you can, diversify your investments and avoid unneeded debt (including higher education, unless it is absolutely required to get where you know you want to be). If you want to become proficient in a business, find a mentor and/or hire a coach in the field. Collaborating with masterminds can stretch you and grow you. TV, video games and other mindless, nonphysical activities do not serve you. If you are looking for a mate, focus more on becoming the partner a successful mate would be seeking than on working your way through dating apps and spending money in bars, restaurants and on entertainment.

If you are in a career, hopefully you already have a mentor. If not, find the most successful person or people in your field and learn from them. Set ambitious goals. Instead of getting too comfortable at one place of employment, find an opportunity to grow, but be mindful of bouncing from job to job every six months to a year (that is called bailing out, not growing). When you are making professional-level money, invest in a professional coach. When you are making executive money, invest in an executive-level coach. Your people deserve you to be an expert in what you do and in leadership. Bring training and resources to the growth of people who matter to you – family members, employees, mentees, non-profits, etc.

If you are an entrepreneur, business owner, or on the executive leadership of a company, as well as doing the above invest in training and resources for your teams. With greater awareness and your trust, your teams will see things that are concerning and escalate them. You investing in them will make them feel valued and appreciated. When they work better together, they will innovate and serve your clients better or more efficiently. Bring in outside experts in business optimisation, market specialists, technology specialists, cybersecurity experts, health and wellbeing experts, etc, that can help improve and grow you and the business. Besides optimising businesses, I also deliver realistic cybersecurity exercises that help teams (including C-suite and board members) experience simulated cyberattack scenarios like ransomware, so that they are not caught unaware and unprepared. Your company is only as strong as its weakest link, and you can actively search for those or you can let them break unexpectedly. Make sure it isn't you.

Finally, get uncomfortable taking care of yourself. Get routine blood tests to check for abnormalities. Find ways to let go of hidden bitterness, anger, unforgiveness, self-judgement, etc. Hire help that improves family and personal quality of life. Do not let comfort blindside you.

Daniel Hammond lives in League City, Texas with his wife, Carolina Batres. He has two amazing adult children, Alex and Maria Gabriella. He and his wife are co-founding members of the LoveLight Campaign for Central America focused on solving root-cause issues of irregular migration in Honduras (Daniel's second home), El Salvador and Guatemala.

Daniel is the president of Ethereal Rodent Cyber Consulting and Cyber Exercise Association – a not for profit company – and a passionate advocate for world-class cyber exercises. He and his partner, Dr Ted Anders, published *Customer Driven Leadership: Legacy Edition,* and through it they deliver powerful organisational transformation. Daniel owns over 700 board games. If you have an impossible problem, reach out to him.

🌐 www.CustomerDrivenLeadership.co

🌐 www.EtherealRodent.com

🌐 https://LoveLightCampaign.org

CHAPTER 6

Disrupt The Education System – Our Future Depends On It

RODDY HERBERT

I can see a world where health and wellbeing and a strong work ethic are mutually inclusive. I imagine a generation that continually innovates, one that's motivated by lifelong learning, with everyone having a value just by being the best they can be. I envisage a community of like-minded souls sharing common values and a belief that 'we are all in it together' for the greater good. That's not where we are right now, nor where we will be in the future if we don't disrupt the content and the way we educate.

We must all take responsibility now to empower young people (YP) to have the emotional resilience for good mental health, the ability to build relationships, flex behaviours and have an innovative mindset that contributes to the future of work (FOW).

YP mental health – do you want to hear some truths?

Mental health is a state of wellbeing in which an individual has the emotional resilience to effectively deal with the normal pressures of life and has the capability to perform at their best in all situations. Everyone has mental health, but it's a continuum from a state of good mental health through to a diagnosis of a mental illness. There is a difference, for example, between feeling anxious and having medically diagnosed anxiety. One is a state of mental health, the other a mental illness.

Schools have a moral and statutory duty of care in the welfare of YP, and in England there's a single point of contact for serious mental health referrals and/or for when a YP is at risk. The remaining YP with mental health issues are expected to be supported by GPs, school nurses and wellbeing champions, as an early intervention.

Here's the shocker: according to The Children's Society, 50% of all mental illnesses (excluding dementia) start before the age of fourteen, and 75% by age eighteen. In 2020, one in six YP aged 5–16 is likely to have experienced a mental health illness in England.[13] That's over one and a quarter million YP!

If this isn't bad enough, the Local Government Association states that mental health services are overstretched, with average waiting times for a YP to see a specialist ranging from fourteen to two hundred days.[14] Around 75% of YP experiencing a mental health problem have to wait so long that their condition gets worse, or they are simply unable to access any treatment at all.

There is a compelling moral, social and economic case for change in the way we support YP with mental health issues.

Education system – does it prepare YP for the future?

The future of every economy and community will be determined by YP and their ability to imagine, innovate

---

13   NHS Digital, Mental Health of Children and Young People in England, 2020: Wave 1 follow up to the 2017 survey (2020), www.digital.nhs.uk/data-and-information/publications/statistical/mental-health-of-children-and-young-people-in-england/2020-wave-1-follow-up, accessed 1 July 2022

14   Paul, N, 'Local Government Association Briefing Initiatives in early intervention in children's lives that would improve the welfare, life chances and social mobility of young people in the UK', Local Government Association (1 November 2018), https://www.local.gov.uk/sites/default/files/documents/1112018%20LGA%20Briefing%20Early%20interventions%20and%20youth%20social%20mobility.pdf, accessed 25 July 2022

and deliver services and products to the global ecosystem. As learning objectives continue to evolve, skills will become the new currency, not content and knowledge.

Many jobs are already being automated. Driverless tractors are ploughing and harvesting our farms. In hospitals, surgery is undertaken using robotics, and in radiology departments AI is used to identify early signs of cancers. There are also driverless robots delivering groceries and small packages to local households. The FOW is here.

Our current education system is a bit like a conveyer belt on a factory production line. Teachers and lecturers stand along its length, with YP the raw material moving down the line, and at each stage YP learn something. As a key performance indicator, 'finished articles' emerge at various end points, having reached a quality standard (or not) determined largely by exam results.

In many instances, this standardised finished article is a square peg trying to fit in a round hole. The education curriculum is dominated by science, technology, engineering and maths (STEM) and the system still views YP's ability to pass various exams as the roadmap to a good job and career.

The FOW does need YP talent with STEM disciplines, but market trends and insights from top global companies all point to a hybrid set of skills as the critical ingredient in the future workforce. These are uniquely human skills such as creativity and innovation, negotiation and persuasion, collaboration and teamwork, and the ability to flex and adapt to change.

Schools are judged, league-tabled and assessed based primarily on exam results. The silo mentality in our education system, with its emphasis on STEM subjects and the reliance on meritocracy in exams as a measure of intelligence and worth, needs to change.

YP emotional resilience – is prevention better than cure?

Having presented keynote speeches and run sessions on emotional resilience for over fifteen years globally to businesses, universities, schools and the NHS, I am an enthusiastic promoter. This enthusiasm is due to the overwhelming scientific evidence behind the many benefits to mental health, wellbeing and cognition that are associated with the techniques I share.

Take as an example the HeartMath Institute's 'heart rhythm biofeedback experience' included in my sessions with YP.[15] Research has consistently shown the many benefits that coherence breathing has, which includes reducing anxiety and improving academic performance.

---

15   Aritzeta, A, et al, 'Reducing Anxiety and Improving Academic Performance Through a Biofeedback Relaxation Training Program', National Library of Medicine (September 2017), https://pubmed.ncbi.nlm.nih.gov/28623467, accessed 25 July 2022

You'd think this evidence would be enough to make protecting the mental health of YP and improving cognitive performance a mandatory component in a school's curriculum, but it's not. The emphasis is still on reacting to mental illness rather than preventing it in the first place. Prevention would reduce human suffering and ease the pressure on mental health services.

There are a number of 'disruptor' educators who have taken the lead and demonstrated new initiatives in YP mental health and wellbeing. With growing academic research demonstrating the wellbeing benefits of mindfulness for YP, in 2010 Tonbridge School led the way in the UK by introducing mindfulness as part of their curriculum. It's estimated that over 370 schools in England have adopted a similar approach, but we need mindfulness to be part of the curriculum in every school, now.

Another disruptor is the Wave Project in Cornwall where 'surf therapy' is used to support YP who face emotional or social challenges. Learning activity is not through traditional routes – one day a week, lessons take place on the beach. The 'Speed Demons' lesson, for example, uses bodyboarding to teach primary school children about maths and physics, with beneficial outcomes. This initiative supports YP by showing them innovative ways they can be motivated to learn, work in teams building relationships, and be a role model to less experienced peers.

Exam meritocracy – is it the only way to value a YP?

YP are subject to extensive testing under the terms of the national curriculum, yet meritocracy based on exam results clearly favours those who are privileged and capable. We are missing the huge potential that YP have when they fall outside this method of measurement. Regarded by many as having the most well-developed education system in the world, Finland has no standardised testing system for YP; rather, students are graded by their teachers and mapped by the Ministry of Education against samples from other school groups.

Meritocracy is a recipe with only one ingredient, but recipes often have ingredients that you can mix and match. A vegetarian can eat a Thai vegetable curry, as opposed to Thai chicken curry. Leaving the chicken out still allows the curry to be flavoursome. What is crucial here is the chef knowing which ingredients and amounts to concentrate on to awaken the consumer's taste buds. For 'chefs' read 'teachers' in an educational setting. Our teachers are stymied to a large extent by having to follow a fairly rigid national curriculum, for which they will be appraised on YP test performances. This is hardly an incentive to promote personalised learning. The education system should be about preparing YP for when they leave academia, and the recipes should not just be flavoursome to YP, but also to prospective employers.

Teachers can encourage YP to thrive in whatever area ignites their interest, and not hold them to strict boundaries on what they must learn. They can nurture, coach and mentor YP to be the best they can be, and recognise that diversity is something to celebrate when developing YP's potential.

According to PwC, by mid-2030 up to 30% of jobs could be replaced by automation.[16] With the FOW being so unpredictable, it must be difficult for YP to find their purpose in how they might contribute to this new world. We need to educate them so they can thrive in it, and we need to allow the huge potential of YP to flourish through the education system.

Capability – are YP fit to undertake FOW demands?

YP are not born 'snowflakes' or with a negative attitude of 'entitlement', but I hear these derogatory remarks aimed at this generation from all walks of life, including employers.

'Snowploughing' is the term used for an intervention to take away or smooth over any life challenges a YP may

---

16   Cameron, E, 'How will automation impact jobs?', PwC (February 2018), www.pwc.co.uk/services/economics/insights/the-impact-of-automation-on-jobs.html, accessed 25 July 2022

face, and snowploughing parents are one factor holding back the potential development of YP in readiness for the FOW. 'Zone of proximal development', in contrast, encourages YP to be exposed to tasks and situations that are challenging, with the guidance of someone with experience – often a teacher, but sometimes a parent or peer. For the sake of the YP, snowploughing parents need to be educated to adopt this rationale. A teacher colleague at an independent school shared with me their experience of being on the receiving end of abuse from a parent whose daughter had been left out of the school hockey team. It would have been helpful for that parent to have appreciated the detrimental effect this response may have had on their child's future ability to deal with life setbacks.

The demand for information and communications technology (ICT) skills from employers is on the increase, yet there is a decline in the number of pupils training in digital skills in education. These skills are crucial for the future of both established and emerging global economies. With self-directed learning being an important lifelong activity, ICT enables YP to explore their own path for knowledge in a creative learning environment and to develop their higher-order thinking skills. To impact YP learning, teachers need to be supported so they can be digitally literate and understand how to integrate ICT learning into the curriculum.

Education disruptors – what's the call to action?

While overnight change to adopt best practice by education policymakers may be a stretch, we can all, as a community or ecosystem, put pressure on those in power to drive the change needed. If we use the example of Sir David Brailsford's success in inspiring peak performance in Britain's Olympic and Team Sky cyclists, we can do this with marginal gains. Here are some suggestions for how this might be achieved:

- Provide a curriculum that enables **emotional resilience** skills learning as a core mandatory subject. With these skills YP can change their behaviour to be proactive in techniques that prevent mental ill health, rather than relying on the current practice of reacting to it.

- Provide a curriculum that has fewer exams, more of a balancing emphasis on **human skills** and less weight on STEM subjects. Using meritocracy linked to exam results in preparation for the FOW fails to recognise full potential, and fails to prepare for the diversity of all the skills that will be needed.

- Provide a **flexible curriculum** that supports teachers in their crucial role of developing every YP to take responsibility for developing their potential to be the best they can be. This can only be done if teachers are truly valued by policymakers and the community, and given adequate free time for continuing personal development and to prioritise their own mental health and wellbeing.

Learning is not the real goal of education. Education should be a means to develop YP to adopt behaviours that have meaning and are fulfilling for both themselves and the community ecosystem they serve.

Roddy Herbert is founder and CEO of Koru International, an international award-winning health and workplace wellness consulting and training firm. Through workshops and speaking engagements, he shares the latest science, research and best practice on achieving high-performance resilience at work with the UK's NHS and educational organisations, and to businesses worldwide.

Professional qualifications and experience in business, coaching and integrative psychotherapeutic counselling give Roddy a valuable perspective on mental health and work/life pressures.

Roddy is also the co-founder of a start-up team of international experts gamifying resilience and high performance for young people. He is passionate that, irrespective of privilege or diversity, all young people should have access to opportunities to learn behaviours that are both emotionally resilient and encourage innovative thinking.

🌐 www.koruinternational.com

🔗 www.linkedin.com/in/roddymacmillanherbert

🐦 https://twitter.com/roddymherbert

✉️ roddy@koruinternational.com

CHAPTER 7

Disrupt Your Marketing
With An App

CHRIS O'HARE

Apps have infiltrated every area of our lives and become the norm for many. You are likely to have at least forty apps on your phone right now, covering everything from food to navigation, music to social media. The app has altered the way we spend our time, with big tech giants using psychological tricks to keep users hooked until they become a cog in their big advertising machine. As highlighted by the Netflix documentary, *The Social Dilemma*, every time you see a notification on an app you are getting a neurochemical 'hit' that makes you feel good. This creates habitual behaviours around phones that we don't see on computers.

Convenient, usually free and accessible to most, the app world has grown into something we risk taking for granted: the Apple App Store has 1.96 million apps and 2.87 million apps are available for download on the Google Play Store.[17] What's more eye-watering is that 21% of millennials open an app fifty-plus times per day, and 49% of all smartphone owners open an app at least eleven times a day. That's a lot of time people are spending on their smartphones and if you're not accessing that market as a business, someone else is: 42% of businesses currently have a mobile app and 30% plan to build one in the future.[18] The humble app can be a powerful ally and disrupt your competition.

In the chapter 'Your Company Is Now A Tech Company', in the book *Success Secrets of Entrepreneurs*, we demonstrated that competitive advantage is a key driver for technological adoption. In this chapter we set about explaining how, more specifically, the app is a big competitive advantage.

17   McCormack, L, 'Mobile App Download Statistics & Usage Statistics (2022)', Buildfire (no date), https://buildfire.com/app-statistics, accessed 5 August 2022

18   Hughart, N, 'The Comprehensive Guide to Business Growth Through Mobile Apps', Buildfire (no date), https://buildfire.com/business-growth-guide-mobile-apps, accessed 5 August 2022

Tech giants own your audience

It's become common knowledge that everything you publish on social media platforms becomes the property of the tech companies. Although this policy feels awkward, it doesn't personally worry me – they can keep my holiday piña colada snaps! It is the implications of the policy that do worry me: those companies have the right to withhold access to that information with no legal recourse.

Imagine you've spent a large amount of time and money trying to increase your audience on one or more of these platforms, which you then become reliant upon to build your business and which becomes your number one pipeline for new work. One day, years after something you said was deemed borderline controversial, someone decides they disagree with you, they report you to the moderators and your account is disabled. You've been retrospectively punished and you have to appeal to get your account back online. Even if you do succeed, that downtime can damage your business. If you diversify your audience across other platforms (often these platforms own others; for example, Facebook owns Instagram and WhatsApp), you may receive a ban on these as well.

Of course, that is the worst-case scenario, but the social media algorithms do have the power to make or break your posts. These algorithms only allow you to reach a small amount of your hard-earned audience, unless they determine you have something exciting to say. They reward content with the shock factor, whether for good or bad. This is frustrating if you just want to talk to your audience as a normal human being. The average engagement rate of a post on Facebook is 0.08% and on LinkedIn it is 0.35%.[19,20]

The same can be said for the search engine Google, that accounts for over 90% of all internet searches in Europe.[21] If Google decides to downgrade your website, your business can be destroyed overnight. I have seen this happen and it isn't so hard to believe when you realise the top three search results get 75.1% of all clicks for that search term.[22]

What's wrong with emails?

You need a way to be able to stay in touch with your audience via more democratic means – this is why marketers always encourage the collection of email addresses so you can contact your audience whenever you please. There are many ways to do this: for example,

19   Aslam, S, '63 Facebook Statistics You Need to Know in 2022', Omnicore (22 February 2022), www.omnicoreagency.com/Facebook-statistics, accessed 5 August 2022

20   Cucu, E, '[STUDY] LinkedIn Engagement Rate: 39,465 Business Posts Show How Visual Oriented Content Gets Ahead on LinkedIn', Social Insider (13 May 2021), www.socialinsider.io/blog/linkedin-engagement-rate, accessed 5 August 2022

21   Mohsin, M, '10 Google Search Statistics You Need To Know in 2022 [INFOGRAPHIC]', Oberlo (2 January 2022), www.oberlo.com/blog/google-search-statistics, accessed 5 August 2022

22   Renderforest Staff, '70+ Google Search Statistics to Know in 2021', Renderforest (2 December 2020), www.renderforest.com/blog/google-search-statistics, accessed 5 August 2022

trading an email address for an eBook or a webinar, although this is a fairly standard exchange that people have become wary of and don't always provide the correct information for.

Once you do have the email address, there is strict governance around not sending the recipient spam. The likes of Mailchimp encourage you to include 'unsubscribe' options and to gain explicit approval from the reader to send to them. If you get through this barrier, your email will receive just a 4.5% open rate at the most.[23] This is primarily because there are many other emails vying for your customers' attention, and because email boxes have become smarter.

Of all email users in the world, 95.2% use five big companies: Gmail, Outlook, Yahoo, NetEase and Tencent (the latter two are Asian companies).[24] Google's Gmail has the majority with 54.4% of all email users. When you have this many users, you can quickly assess people's behaviour by the way they interact with a particular email and score its authenticity.

New spam-filtering technology using AI has increased filtering to a new level, shuttling any emails that may

---

23   Reckless, 'Email vs Push Notifications vs In-App Messaging: Which has the highest engagement?', Reckless (no date), https://reckless.agency/insight/email-vs-push-notifications-vs-in-app-messaging-which-has-the-highest-engagement, accessed 5 August 2022

24   Statistics & Data, 'Most Popular Email Providers in History', Statistics & Data (no date), https://statisticsanddata.org/data/most-popular-email-providers-in-history, accessed 5 August 2022

contain marketing to a 'low priority' or 'other' box, which means your email will likely be unnoticed and your customers will focus on more pressing emails. As a premillennial invention, emails are still great for communication – but not for marketing.

Marketing, amplified

People view apps as a utility tool, when in fact they're a powerful marketing tool. When using an app for marketing, the mentality of the customer is reversed: you're providing value rather than selling to them. They become intrigued about what's in store when they download the app. Requiring a sign-up to access the app increases the likelihood of the customers passing over their correct details, while being on the app stores increases your credibility and helps them to trust that you will use their details for legitimate purposes.

Even if your only goal is to improve the quality of your email addresses, an app is one of the most effective ways to do so. The average chance of getting a customer to sign up to a newsletter is only 1.95%, compared with the average download rate of an app of 30.3%.[25] This makes an app eleven times more effective of the two.

As a way of collecting all your marketing content, the app

25   Peterson, S, 'Email Signup Benchmarks: How Many Visitors Should Be Converting', Sumo (22 April 2019), https://sumo.com/stories/email-signup-benchmarks, accessed 5 August 2022

can be incredibly helpful for your customer. By providing them with eBooks, cheat sheets, podcasts, tutorials or anything else you think they might benefit from, the app allows your customer to get all the information they could want from you in one place.

Once you know more about the customer from their behaviour on the app, the pages they're interested in and the information they've provided, the app can go one step further by personalising the content shown to them. This tailored experience has been proven to increase the likelihood of a purchase by 80%. On the flip side, in a world where content is so widely available, 74% of customers feel frustrated with the brand if the marketing content hasn't been personalised.[26]

The power of push notifications

The often-overlooked power of an app is its ability to send push notifications. Push notifications are the alerts that appear on your smartphone when you receive a message from an app. They look similar to the notifications you receive with an SMS message and have the same visibility, but they have one key difference: the user doesn't have to provide a phone number to receive this notification but is still notified with as much importance as if they had. If you've ever received an unsolicited text message,

26   Kazi, R, 'The state of inbound', Digital 22 (no date), www.digital22.com/insights/the-state-of-inbound-marketing, accessed 5 August 2022

it feels like a violation of your privacy; somehow, a push notification doesn't.

The push notification taps into your customers' neuro-chemical reward centres, which have already been built by other smartphone behaviours: your customers will feel an urge to read your notification. The open rate goes from 4.5% for emails to 45% for push notifications; nearly half of your audience will view that notification and, unlike SMS notifications, push notifications are free.[27]

The power of the push notification cannot be overstated: it gives you the authority to mobilise your audience all at once. One way this has been used effectively is to overcome the barrier of social media algorithms by alerting your audience when you post new content, creating a need to see what you've posted. Your audience is also likely to support you by liking and commenting, boosting the social media post with organic growth to other parts of the network and increasing its visibility.

Because the smartphone is a personal device, push notifications create a personal interaction with the customer that you're communicating with, especially if the notification is personalised using their name and the content they're interested in. With regular notifications, you're able to reinforce your brand and stay

---

27   Rose, C, 'Benefits Of Push Notifications & How It Improves Your App', Squash Apps (8 August 2021), https://squashapps.com/blog/benefits-of-push-notifications, accessed 5 August 2022

in the forefront of the customer's mind. The 'effective frequency' of how often your customers have to see your brand before making a purchase is twenty times.

Like most marketing techniques, this all comes with the caveat that you need to ensure your audience values what you're sending them. That's why some apps create seven-day learning programmes that reinforce your customers' habitual behaviours, turning your marketing funnel into a learning experience. Customers don't want to be sold to, they want to be taught, and the app is the perfect place to do this.

Change your customer's perspective

As common as apps have become, customers still hold the view that having your own app is a big deal and increases your credibility as a business owner. One study found that customers who interacted with a business with a perceived high level of technology were more likely to become engaged and as a result spend 300% more than customers who did not.[28] Hypnotherapist Dipti Tait summed this up: 'New clients treat me differently now, they're always awed that I have an app and I definitely have an advantage compared to other hypnotherapists. One customer said, "It's very reassuring to have Dipti in my pocket."'

---

28   Scott Gould, 'Engagement Statistics', Scott Gould (29 January 2018), https://scottgould.me/engagement-statistics, accessed 5 August 2022

To be in your customer's pocket when they need you is a powerful psychological prompt; it's reassuring, and you've moved them from logical decision-making using the head, to their intuitive sense of 'it feels right'. Harvard professor Gerald Zaltman says 95% of all purchasing decisions are controlled by the buyer's gut feeling.[29]

There are several ways to get your customer to 'trust their gut'. One of these is to de-risk purchasing from you. The easiest way to do that is to provide a lower-priced product so they can try you and your services. Often an app can be the low-risk first purchase. Over time, as that trust is established, they will buy more from you at an increased price.

Another way is to use impulse purchases by providing an offer via a push notification to upgrade, book or purchase before the offer runs out. In one study, 53.3% of consumers agreed that most purchases made using smartphones were impulse buys.[30] Impulse purchases are not as impulsive as you'd believe; the customer has built trust and familiarity with the brand over time and if they make a purchase it's because they trust their gut and just need an offer to push them over the line. The app enables its users to react to the offer and purchase with

29   Chierotti, L, 'Harvard Professor Says 95% of Purchasing Decisions Are Subconscious', Inc, (no date), www.inc.com/logan-chierotti/harvard-professor-says-95-of-purchasing-decisions-are-subconscious.html, accessed 5 August 2022

30   Skeldon, P, 'Mobile News', Internet Retailing (19 March 2019), https://internetretailing.net/magazine-article/mobile-news-march-2019, accessed 5 August 2022

ease, especially when they're outside their typical work environment and are not looking at their emails.

When integrated into an ecosystem of technology, the app is an incredible cog in the flywheel to engage your audience with push notifications before converting them into customers with a purchase. Disrupt your marketing with an app.

Chris O'Hare is the founder of Hare Digital, a digital strategy and app development agency that has worked with numerous brands, including BIP100, Royal Mail and BMW.

Hare Digital provides a chief technology officer for hire service alongside building complex web applications, mobile applications, workflow automation and emerging technologies, including IoT, blockchain and AI.

Chris has been a developer for more than ten years and gained a first-class bachelor's degree, and a master's degree with distinction in computer science with business, from the University of Sussex. He has also received multiple awards for his achievements and for his business from the university and from Brighton's business awards.

Chris's ability to translate technical jargon and problems into understandable concepts before applying them to business models relevant to the audience has been noted by many business leaders.

🌐 www.hare.digital/disrupt-your-marketing-with-an-app

🌐 www.hare.digital/podcast

🌐 www.hare.digital/social

CHAPTER 8

Disruptors In The Stock Market

OWEN O'MALLEY

Most people fail miserably to become financially free. Many try by trading the stock market, but only a few succeed. Those of us who do, make annual returns that we aim to achieve... monthly. Keep reading to see how we do this or, if you are more of a visual person, watch the videos referenced at the end of this chapter.

Since 1792, when the New York Stock Exchange began, most investors in the stock market have simply bought and sold shares. Of the more than one billion shares traded every day, the average buy-and-hold period is six months, dramatically lower than the average of eight years in the 1950s. The greatest advocator for buy-and-hold is Warren Buffett, born in 1930 and worth US$125 billion, who started with an investment of US$110 at age eleven in 1942.

In 1973, a new trading instrument was invented in the Chicago Board Options Exchange (CBOE) called 'equity option'. Equity options were, and are still, seen as major disruptors to the stock exchange. In this essay we will explore how equity options disrupt and add value to the stock market. More importantly, we will show you how you can use equity options to become wealthy.

Only 10% of shares in the market have issued equity options and many of the companies that have use employee share option schemes to retain and motivate their staff. When successful, these schemes add great value while helping many employees become financially free.

In 2022, Walmart has 2.3 million employees who collectively own 48.3% of the company, worth US$204 billion. The average value of the shareholding per employee is around US$90,000.[31] There are examples of people retiring from Walmart today who are worth more than US$1 million, having stacked shelves for many years.

---

31   Downing, K, 'API Report', Value Line (22 April 2022), www.valueline.com

This is all thanks to the disruptor vision of the Walmart founder, Sam Walton, who insisted, from the beginning, that all Walmart employees deducted 6% of their wage to buy Walmart shares. What vision and commitment he demonstrated to add value to his precious employees.

There are two types of equity options traded on the CBOE: call options and put options.

Call options

In our investment clubs, we sell call options to generate an income from our shares. By selling call options over and over, we eventually own our shares for free – just like you might buy a house and rent it until it is paid for. Rental property can take up to twenty to thirty years to be self-financed from the rental income. In some of our investment clubs, we self-finance the purchase of our shares in two to three years. With these figures, we can say our clubs do ten times the return on investment (ROI) with respect to property. But what is a 'call option'?

For the buyer, a call option is an option to buy a share at an agreed price on or before a fixed time and date called 'expiration'. The seller, who owns the shares, receives a payment, called 'premium', to allow the buyer to buy the shares at the agreed price any time before the expiration.

Monthly options expire on the third Friday of the month at 4pm Eastern Standard Time. The buyer of a call option has the right, but not the obligation, to call the share from the seller of that call option any time up to that deadline. The seller of a call option is obliged, if called upon to do so, to deliver the shares to the buyer of the call option at the pre-agreed price, known as 'strike price', any time between the date sold and the expiry date and time.

Equity call options are seen as a great way of accumulating shares in the future at a fixed price. Long-term equity options expire within twenty-eight months of being issued. Any option that will expire more than nine months from the date of issue is termed as a 'long-term equity accumulation plan'. They are used by many to pay a small amount to lock in a guaranteed purchase price in the future.

Put options

For the buyer, a 'put option' is an option to sell shares for an agreed price on or before the expiry date. People usually buy put options to protect their shares from a drop in price in the future. The buyers of put options are prepared to pay a premium at the time of purchase to insure themselves against a potential drop in value in the future.

In our investment clubs, we do the opposite: we sell put options to be able to buy shares we would like to own today for a discounted price in the future. We are like an insurance company in that we collect premiums from the buyers of put options.

When we sell put options, there are only six possible outcomes:

1. If the share price ends up above the strike price on the expiry date, we get to keep the premium and no further action is required.

2. If the share price ends up below the strike price on the expiration day, we can choose to allow the shares to be put to us at a discounted price.

3. If the share price rises significantly above the strike price before the expiry date, we can buy back the put option for less than we received to make a profit. We aim to give back 20% of the premium, keeping 80%. This action of buying back the put option early, before the expiry date, allows us to reuse and recycle the buying power to sell another put option.

4. If it looks like the share price will end up below the strike price on the expiration date, we can push forward the put option. To do this in the one trade, we buy back the current month's put option and sell a future put option for a net credit.

5. If shares are put to us prematurely and we don't wish to own them, we can sell the shares back to the market and then sell a future put for a net credit. This is the same net result as above except,

in this case, the shares were put to us earlier than expected.

6. If the share price rises, we can buy a lower strike price protective put option for the same expiration date for a fraction of the cost compared to our income. We typically offer 10% to buy our own protective put option, thereby keeping 90% of the original premium collected. We engineer the trade to make sure that the 90% net credit is greater than the net loss if both put options are exercised on the expiration date.

We see options as a powerful way to disrupt the normal stock market per annum returns. What the buy-and-holders would consider as a good per annum ROI, we would consider as a satisfactory per month ROI.

Compound interest wheels

How do we, and more importantly how could you, achieve exceptional monthly returns? We employ five compound interest wheels in our investment system which we can teach you so you can learn how to apply the same system for yourself.

1. Compounded earnings growth

2. Reinvesting collected call options premium

3. Reinvesting collected put option premium

4. Reinvesting dividend income

5. Recycling and reusing surplus buying power

1. Compound earnings growth

We only buy the strongest companies in the world when they present excellent value. These companies use the power of compound interest growth by reinvesting their profits to increase the strength of their balance sheet. We enjoy exceptional long-term buy-and-hold value increase over time.

2. Reinvesting collected call options premium

When shares are at high points in their long-term growth cycle, we sell call options to collect a call option income. We use this call option income to buy other shares at low points. The new shares also yield an option income, which we use to buy more income-producing shares. This repeating process allows us to tap into the power of compound interest.

3. Reinvesting collected put option premium

When shares are at low points in their long-term growth cycle, we sell put options to generate put option income. We use this put option income to buy other shares at low points. Once again, the new shares yield an option income which we use to buy more income-producing shares, and the process has a compounding effect.

4. Reinvesting dividend income

Not every share will pay dividends. For those that do, we collect the dividend income to buy more shares at low points. Some of those shares in turn pay a dividend, and we are now making income on income, which is exactly what compound interest growth is.

5. Recycling and reusing surplus buying power

For every dollar we lodge into our online share-dealing broker account, the clearing firm offers us the facility to invest two dollars. This is known as a 'margin facility'. The broker can charge up to 7% interest if you choose to use the margin facility.

We have a clever way to use the margin facility for free: we make promises to buy shares (that we do not plan to buy) in the future at low prices by selling put options, and collect the corresponding put option premium. To keep this trading activity safe, we only use 30–50% of the margin loan facility.

First, we sell a naked put option, which means the shares could be put to us in the future at the strike price we agree to buy the shares for. The next step is to place a proactive, protective trade. The proactive, protective trade consists of buying a put option at the strike price below the naked put option we sold.

When we place the proactive, protective trade, we will typically offer 10% of the previous premium we received when we sold the naked put. This way, if the share price ends up above the strike price on the expiration date we sold the put for, we get to keep 90% of the original premium collected.

If the share price ends up below the lower put option strike that we bought, we will only lose the difference between the strike price put option we sold and the strike price put option we bought. If the net income from selling the higher put option strike price and buying the lower put option strike price is greater than the net risk of the two trades, we will have created a zero-cost and zero-risk trade.

This combination trade of the two put options is known as a credit 'bull put spread'. The most powerful aspect of this zero-risk and zero-cost trade is that we release 90% of the buying power to be reused and recycled in another powerful trade.

Because we create a production line of both naked puts and covered put spreads that will expire over the upcoming months, we give shares plenty of time to grow and release more buying power before the expiration dates.

We've shared some detailed and complicated information with you... now you can relax. You might want to join an investment club, which is a safe and supportive environment for you to learn and powerfully grow both your money and your knowledge.

Here are 5 very short 2-minute videos to help you understand our trading system:

1. www.tinyurl.com/4interest

2. www.tinyurl.com/ticnassets

3. www.tinyurl.com/bupsbups

4. www.tinyurl.com/putsputs

5. www.tinyurl.com/calloptions

To test drive one of our investment clubs or work with us one on one, please, send an email to ana@ticn.ie and we will help get you started on your journey to financial freedom.

Owen O'Malley is on a thirty-year mission to create one million millionaires using the powerful global stock market as a vehicle. He has initiated over 1,000 investment clubs in fifty-two different countries, and educated over 25,000 people in fifteen different languages.

Owen has authored and co-authored ten books and has spoken at many large global events. He has been interviewed on national radio and television and has built a powerful team of educators and traders, teaching people to make their money work harder.

Owen and his team have also empowered teenagers to understand how the global stock markets work. His purpose and passion is to bring financial literacy skills to this and future generations.

 www.ticn.ie

 www.linkedin.com/in/owenomalleyshares

CHAPTER 9

Music: The Land Of The Free

BARRY PAISLEY

If you look back into history, you will see that most of the figureheads we look up to are disruptors who changed the norm. From Martin Luther King, who fought for civil rights, to Bob Marley, who conquered the world through his music, these individuals opened minds and changed the world.

I explored the world of music as I felt it was the land of the free. For me, being an artist was the opposite to the structure-following world of education and therefore somewhat radical. Working within the industry,

I experienced first-hand that this is not the case. Aged nineteen I was offered my first record deal, and what stood out the most was the length of the document filled with rules and regulations, which included the record label having full control over my image. My initial thought was, 'So I don't control what I look like?' As a young man at the start of my independence, this was a major turn-off which eventually led to me declining the deal. I saw the industry in a new light; I realised that my favourite musicians all had contracts and were slaves to the terms and conditions.

Constantly listening to the radio and watching music videos sparked multiple questions: 'I wonder what deal they signed? What regulations are they under? Are they happy?' I remember reading an article about the musician Prince, who went as far as changing his name in 1993 just to avoid the hold the record label Warner Brothers had on his career. Prince didn't stop there: he wrote the word 'slave' on his face during performances, highlighting to the world that when you sign the wrong contract that is exactly what you are. Musicians and labels ended up in legal battles for a number of reasons, from unpaid royalties to unscrupulous business practices. I watched one of my favourite R&B groups, TLC, go bankrupt while their music grossed millions. At the same time, I learned many signed artists end up in debt to the recording labels.

The impact of social media

Then came social media, which was an incredible tool for creators. This seemed like freedom: by 2008 Myspace and Facebook had reached an incredible 115 million users. YouTube took over video consumption, the industry migrated to digital and we could finally share our content directly to the consumer. Content started to go viral without being tied to a contract – artists like Justin Bieber and Soulja Boy rose to fame from simple videos recorded with a camcorder. For a while, record labels struggled to compete with the emerging trend of independent artists and musicians who didn't need record deals to become famous.

Many went on to sign deals but were in a far better position by having already obtained a fan base online. Others stayed independent by expanding into merch and independent tours to fund their careers. A shift occurred; labels no longer had the power they once did to control creators. With music becoming digital, labels also lost their hold on the product. It was a double-edged sword: musicians became viral sensations but their content was being digested for free via online torrents and the ability to illegally download.

After a while, we experienced the emergence of streaming platforms by the likes of Napster, Apple (who acquired Napster) and Spotify, to name a few, which brought back some value to what had become an industry of free music. It was not long before the consumer devalued the notion of becoming viral. Attention spans shortened and after a few days not many people cared if you had a million views. Social media and streaming platforms like YouTube began to exploit their positions, grossing the most but paying the least while forcing creators into paid advertisements for visibility. According to Statista, in 2020 Meta (formerly Facebook) made 97.9% of its income via digital advertisements.[32] The introduction of algorithms that affect viewings made it difficult for creators with less engagement than popular artists who published a post at the same time. Ironically, a timeline became nothing to do with time.

Behind the scenes, music industry executives like Lyor Cohen earned influential positions in platforms like YouTube, which highlighted to me that social media had slowly become what record labels once were by having a strong hold on a musician's success. Spotify started signing creators exclusively in exchange for reach. Most recently, after signing a two-year deal, Joe Budden ridiculed Spotify for undervaluing his number one podcast while offering others like Joe Rogan a reported US$200 million dollars across three and a half years.

---

32   Dixon, S, 'Meta: advertising revenue worldwide 2009–2021',Statista (18 February 2022), www.statista.com/statistics/271258/facebooks-advertising-revenue-worldwide, accessed 18 July 2022

The advent of blockchain and nonfungible tokens

While the digital era matured, a decentralised network developed in the background. This came to be known as the blockchain. It started as a revolutionary way to send and receive digital currency in the form of tokens, with the pioneer being Bitcoin. For the first time, we did not need a centralised entity to make transactions, and we no longer needed permission from a set of individuals to transfer wealth. These transactions were open, transparent and required consensus from random nodes around the world. Anyone could set up a node to verify currency sent from one person to another while earning rewards known as 'mining'. At the heart of all business lies a transaction, and now that we had the ability to trade without the need of a gatekeeper, the disruption began. In 2014 Ethereum launched as the second public blockchain. Adding to what Bitcoin initially provided, Ethereum offered a faster and more advanced network that gave us the ability to build websites and programs around the original element of decentralised transactions.

This initiated the birth of a new generation of music platforms that essentially cut out the go-betweens, offering artists more revenue per stream than traditional Web 2.0 platforms. One of the first to do this was Audius, who offered 90% of income to the artists while the remaining 10% went to node operators, no record label needed. Finally, the idea of true direct-to-consumer began to circle the minds of the intuitive. Freedom from the point of creation to distribution was now a possibility.

During 2020 a new trend occurred on the blockchain in the form of nonfungible tokens (NFTs). This was not a new concept as the first NFT was created in 2014 by digital artist Kevin McCoy. It was essentially a pixelated image of an octagon but eventually became seen as a way to digitise an asset. Art was the first industry to be disrupted by NFTs. The art industry had a number of issues, the first of which was accessibility as the sale of art has always been a niche market. Proving the authenticity of art can also be expensive, with buyers reliant on other entities to validate legitimacy.

NFTs are tokens on the blockchain that are not much different from fungible tokens such as Bitcoin or Ethereum. The incredible thing about a token on the blockchain is that it can't be replicated: once copied it becomes a whole new asset. You'll never come across a fake Bitcoin; all data is open, transparent and recorded. This is also true of NFTs. If an artist mints 100 copies of a painting (as an NFT), only 100 would ever exist. This sparked an interest not only from art collectors but collectors in general. By simply right-clicking to save an image, you are not the owner of the asset as you do not possess the token, you've simply got a JPEG with no value. By contrast, as NFTs are digital, the world now has access to your art, opening the market to buyers from all around the world. As a programmable asset, artists now have the ability to attach a royalty fee to ensure that the creator earns a percentage every time the art is sold on, forever. This is not true of conventional art, which led many artists down the rabbit hole of tokenisation.

New creative ideas

While artists raked in millions, other genres of the creative arts, including the music industry, eagerly watched from the sidelines. Individuals like myself had the idea of minting audio as tokens. Minds began to tick: what would this look like for us? In 2020 I sketched out many ideas, one being fractionalised ownership of songs in the form of NFTs. What if fans shared ownership and earnings with musicians; would this incentivise a lost emotional connection between musician and consumer? With the introduction of reality TV and the saturation of available music, I personally felt that musicians were no longer larger than life. The days of a Michael Jackson-type superfan fainting at a concert were few and far between. People enjoyed their favourite music but were no longer deeply connected. In 2021 a platform called Royal, created by DJ 3LAU, achieved just that. Fans could now share ownership with music artists via NFTs, American rapper Nas being one of the first to take advantage of this.

In late 2019 a good friend of mine, Greg, educated me on the Internet Computer Protocol (ICP), a new blockchain developed by the DFINITY Foundation. Though other chains have existed in between, ICP is considered the third generation in blockchain development, with Bitcoin and Ethereum being the first and second. In June 2020 I had the pleasure of joining one of DFINITY's online events. For the first time I experienced what it looked like to be able to store assets 100% on chain. Though NFTs have previously been minted on networks like Ethereum, the associated media has not – it was merely linked to the earlier NFTs via a uniform resource identifier. Media had previously been stored elsewhere on alternative decentralised storage networks like the InterPlanetary File System (IPFS) and Filecoin, which exist to store files that could not be stored on the associated blockchains. It currently costs US$20k to store 500kb on Ethereum. I realised I was now part of a deeper disruption – building on ICP we were now disrupting the disruptors. What could I do with this technology?

I had already had the idea of protecting copyrights and digital intellectual property (IP). Creators currently store their digital IP on hard drives, computers and centralised clouds, all of which carry the risk of losing access to your content in one way or another. If lost, how will you prove ownership? Storing your files 100% on chain is the perfect solution as there is no risk of damaging hardware, the time stamp is transparent, authenticated and stored in the most secure fashion to date. This idea birthed what was to become Canistore, a social media platform with a licensing protocol at heart. Canistore allows creators to upload, create a licence and store content directly on the blockchain, while boasting the usual functionality and engagement of familiar Web 2.0 platforms such as Instagram, Spotify and Facebook. The ICP opened my eyes to the most disruptive aspect: governance. Platforms like Canistore are now community-owned and community-governed.

Web 3.0

Token holders now have voting power similar to shares in equity. Users in general have a say on the decisions made regarding the future of the platform. The days of Web 2.0 platforms like YouTube making decisions without the community are coming to an end. We are in the realm of technological democracy; you'll no longer receive an update on your app that the community did not ask for. We build apps and services for the community, with the community. Web 3.0 is the future and is already changing how we interact and digest content; if you are a creator, I urge you to explore.

I'd like to share with you a breakdown of the evolution of the web as first explained to me by a good friend and tokenomics specialist, Mo Ezeldin. Web 1.0 = Read. Web 2.0 = Read and Write. Web 3.0 (blockchain) = Read, Write and Own. In true blockchain fashion, I am available and currently building with the community. Feel free to contact me for a chat about anything from blockchain to music. Don't be shy, I don't always bite.

Barry Paisley is a visionary and democratic CEO, and the entrepreneur navigating the Canistore helm. With over two decades of experience in the music and entertainment industry, Barry's knowledge of business conception, perseverance and sustainability has served him well in establishing companies specialising in a variety of fields, from graphic design to blockchain technology.

Barry's father penned for the late Smiley Culture of 80s fame. As a recording artist, songwriter and producer himself, and not averse to the wants and needs of an artist, Barry knows only too well the failings of the industry. Barry has a degree in audio production, a background in marketing and visual editing (Bushbash Recordings and Sky TV), has managed the successful London nightclub 'Nomad', and has established three recording studios. His expertise is indicative of the success of Canistore and the disruption it will bring to the music business.

🌐 http://canistore.io

in https://uk.linkedin.com/in/barrypaisley

🐦 https://twitter.com/BHYPEMUSIC

📷 www.instagram.com/bhypemusic

CHAPTER 10

Riding The Waves
Of Disruption

PAULA PETRY

We are at the end of an era. Globally, disruptive waves are in motion, creating a disequilibrium which impacts everyone everywhere. The pendulum has swung out of balance and is seeking homeostasis. It is a time of the Great Turning, as described by climate activist Joanna Macy.[33] New life-sustaining regenerative systems in economics, the judiciary, education, agriculture and

---

33   Macy, J R, *Stories of a Great Turning* (Vala Publishing Cooperative Ltd, 2013)

health are needed – systems that maximise long-term benefits for people and nature. If we don't want to be engulfed, learning to ride the waves of disruption is more important now than ever.

The effects of the disequilibrium are reflected in the mental health status of the USA. An estimated 20% of adults have a mental illness, almost 10% of youth suffer from severe depression, 4% with a substance use disorder.[34] Between 1999 and 2019, the suicide death rate in the USA increased by 33%.[35] Provisional data from the Center for Disease Control and Prevention's National Center for Health Statistics indicates that in one year, between 2020 and 2021, there was an increase of 28.5% in drug overdose deaths.[36]

As if to mirror our emotional wellbeing, our dear planet Earth is also suffering. Her waters are contaminated; somewhere along the line we made it OK to dump our waste into her oceans, rivers and lakes, adding to the over 2 billion people lacking access to clean water. Her skies are polluted; the toxins we breathe are causing illness and disease. Her forests are disappearing, exacerbating

---

34   Mental Health America, '2021 The State of Mental Health in America', www.mhanational.org/research-reports/2021-state-mental-health-america, accessed 20 October 2022

35   United Health Foundation, America's Health Rankings, Annual Report, www.americashealthrankings.org/explore/annual/measure/Suicide/state/ALL, accessed 1 July 2022

36   Centers for Disease Control and Prevention, 'Drug Overdose Deaths in the U.S. Top 100,000 Annually', www.cdc.gov/nchs/pressroom/nchs_press_releases/2021/20211117.htm, accessed 1 July 2022

climate change, soil erosion and flooding, and increasing the amount of greenhouse gases in the atmosphere.

Growing and evolving into a better way of being can build resiliency – but how? The answer is embedded in the ancient healing traditions, quantum field theory and the specific practices they each support. I know this to be true not only as a scientist but as a shamanic energy medicine practitioner, and as a mother who desperately sought this wisdom.

My 12-year-old daughter's sudden death, in 1996, and my subsequent divorce left me in a puddle of despair and fear; the world as I knew it had shattered. Rebuilding was a painstakingly slow process that included five years of psychoanalysis to reclaim a sense of identity. Later, seeking answers to life's big questions, I resigned from my faculty position at the medical school, sold my home, and gave almost everything away. I stepped into the void, an adventure I describe in my memoir, *A Mother's Courage to Awaken*.[37]

Amid this cataclysm, the world waiting for me unfolded. Completely by accident I met the people, Bert Farr and Alberto Villoldo, who held the wisdom I was seeking. I studied the Akashic records, the source of cosmic knowledge, shamanic energy medicine, sound healing, and the science that supports each one. I travelled to

---

37   Petry, P, *A Mother's Courage to Awaken* (Mango Publishing House, 2020)

Peru and studied with the Q'ero shamans and climbed their sacred mountains. In upstate New York I joined a sweat lodge, which led to creating holistic wellbeing programmes for adults, youth and teachers.

After years of rigorous evaluation of my courses and retreats, I am confident that following the recommendations based on the precepts of holistic wellbeing I describe below will help you safely ride the waves of disruption into the future.

Spend time with nature

Planet Earth lives within us and we live within her. Our ability to love and take care of ourselves mirrors our ability to love and care for her. To ride the waves of disruption, we must develop an earth-human partnership; otherwise, we will continue to suffer. Her air is our breath. Her earth is our body. Her waters reside in our every cell. Her fire is the life-force that fuels us.

Love and appreciation for planet Earth grows from spending time together. Attention is a form of love. Examine a leaf for what feels to be a long time, listen intently to a water stream, sit at the base of a tree and imagine melding with it. Be curious about the Earth's cycles and patterns, subtle shifts during seasonal changes, and the movement and shapes in her sky. Perhaps even dialogue with the Earth's other species. Ceremonially offer a sprinkling of tobacco. These exchanges bring rich and transformative discoveries on how consciousness lives in all the species.

According to environmental medicine research,[38] being in nature has significant health benefits. Studies measuring the impact of earthing or grounding – having direct skin contact with the earth – show that simply touching the earth with our hands or feet changes physiology and health. In a recent study, grounding was shown to improve sleep, normalise the day–night cortisol rhythm, and shift the autonomic nervous system from sympathetic towards parasympathetic, positively affecting wound healing and inflammation.[39] Earthing advocates remind us that our once-natural leather-soled shoes are now rubber, further distancing us from the earth's magnetic field and contributing to our deteriorating health and wellbeing.

Awaken to the interconnectedness of all life

Begin to question the human story. Reductionism and Western medicine have focused us on isolated parts rather than interconnected systems working together holistically. This perspective has contributed to competition, greed,

38   Menigoz, W, Latz, TT, Ely, RA, Kamei, C, Melvin, G, & Sinatra, D, 'Integrative and lifestyle medicine strategies should include Earthing (grounding): Review of research evidence and clinical observations', *Explore*, (2020) 16(3), 152-160

39   Chevalier, G, Sinatra, ST, Oschman, JL, Sokal, K, Sokal, P, 'Earthing: Health implications of reconnecting the human body to the Earth's surface electrons', J Environ Public Health, 291541 (2012), www.hindawi.com/journals/jeph/2012/291541, accessed 1 July 2022

runaway consumerism and the plundering of Earth's resources.

I urge you to consider the existence of what Native Americans refer to as the web of life, in which we are all connected through nature. Through this lens, community is more important than the individual, creating a safety net for all. There is no subjugation of one species by another but rather a constant striving to live in balance.

The web of life is proving to be real. Science is substantiating the existence of a unifying quantum field. This force field is said to have intelligence and interacts with all life forms. In this, every atom inside of us is connected to the rest of the universe we move through. This means that everything we do impacts the collective – not just ourselves. When one feels, we all feel. There is no separation between you and other. This lens promotes what is now most needed: restorative circles, living economies, shared decision-making, preserving and honouring planet Earth and her natural resources, and thoughtful leadership that recognises the importance of the balance between all that is.

Realise that perception shapes life

How friendly do you perceive the universe to be? Albert Einstein considered the most important question humanity could ask itself: 'Is the universe a friendly place?'.[40] 'The answer we find determines what we do with our entire lives,' he explained in an interview. If we decide the universe is friendly, we spend our time building bridges. If we decide the opposite, we spend our time building walls, using our resources to destroy all that we perceive to be unfriendly. He advised to adopt this perspective; uncertainty needs to become our friend.

Dr Alberto Villoldo, medical anthropologist and founder of The Four Winds Society, a shamanic energy medicine programme, shares a similar truth arising from dialogues with the wisdomkeepers, the Q'ero shamans of Peru. Their message was that although there will be no completely safe places, there are safe people.[41,42] The shaman and the physicist are telling us that safety is an inside job.

Learn practices to build safety from within

How do we become 'safe people'? How do we perceive the world as friendly, no matter what? Dr Villoldo teaches that it begins by making the conscious effort to reset one's autonomic system by turning off the fight, flight, or freeze response. Though this hyper alert state exists in all species,

40   Atkinson, M, 'A Life Lesson From Einstein', Erickson Coaching International (28 August 2012), https://marilynatkinson.erickson.edu/blog/einstein-on-the-porch, accessed 2 August 2022

41   The Four Winds, www.thefourwinds.com, accessed 6 July 2022

42   Villoldo, A, 'Creating SAFETY' (2020) www.youtube.com/watch?v=49AqjTuBSkw, accessed 1 August 2022

humans are the only ones that do not automatically reset once the threat is over.

Our amygdala, the almond-like shape part of our brain, is what activates the body's sympathetic system – turning on the body's fight, flight or freeze response. In this high-alert state, the brain's prefrontal cortex – the part that helps us reason, plan and problem-solve, and gives us impulse-control – is necessarily turned off. This leaves our impulsive, irrational primitive brain in charge. When stress is chronic, the cortisol hormone released during this stress response continues to flow, affecting short- and long-term memory, and disrupting the body's ability to return to homeostasis, making it increasingly difficult for the body to heal and restore.

Riding the waves must include simple techniques to help return the body to homeostasis, to turn off the sympathetic system, and to activate the parasympathetic. Such techniques are found in ancient practices and supported by modern science.

Stimulate your vagus nerve

The vagus nerve is the largest and most important nerve in the body, running from your brain all the way to your large intestine. It is referred to as a 'wandering nerve' and its existence is documented all the way back to ancient times. When it is stimulated, the sympathetic system turns off and the parasympathetic system is activated. Here are five effective ways to stimulate your vagus nerve:

1. Cold water immersion. Place an ice pack on your face or neck, or begin or end your day with a cold shower.

2. Chanting, singing or humming. The vagus nerve is connected to the vocal cords and the muscles in the neck.

3. Lying on the right-hand side of the body. Lying on one's left side is not as effective and lying on one's back decreases vagus nerve stimulation.

4. Foot massage with a gentle or strong touch. In traditional Chinese medicine, reflexology puts pressure on specific acupressure points in the hands and feet to improve the function of our glands, organs and central nervous system, and to alleviate stress.

5. Meditation with a focus on deep rhythmic breathing. There are numerous apps to guide meditation and breathing practices.

As this wheel of change slowly turns, it is critical that we learn how to move with the wheel so as not to get caught beneath it. This means embracing uncertainty and keeping fear and worry at a distance. It means learning about the unifying force field and its relationship with planet Earth, ourselves and each other. Riding the wheel of change means consciously resetting our autonomic nervous system by engaging in daily restorative practices. As we disengage from fear and worry and maintain a routine to reset, our 'the universe is friendly' lens becomes stronger and stronger. Living with one's default lens set to friendly helps ensure that the bridge we are collectively building into the future is worthy of the tremendous pain and suffering necessary for its construction.

Dr Paula Petry's work is motivated by her deep desire for a world where all beings feel safe, loved and nourished. Her compassion and wisdom spawn from her profound suffering after the loss of her daughter, Alexandra. Paula's healing journey took her into the unordinary. Desperately seeking answers, she resigned from her long-standing faculty position at the University of Miami's School of Medicine, sold her home and gave almost everything away.

Paula has studied ancient shamanic healing traditions, quantum field theory and the specific practices they support. Her conviction that today's individual and collective solutions lie in these teachings forms the foundation of her transformational courses, presentations and shamanic energy medicine sessions. Her journey is described in her memoir, *A Mother's Courage to Awaken*.

🌐 www.paulapetry.com

in www.linkedin.com/in/paula-petry-phd-a1267711

CHAPTER 11

Wellbeing Is The Future Of Work

SARAH PIDDINGTON

The future of work has been disrupted. When we emerged from two years of living in a world centred around Covid-19, we discovered that the world had changed. Today, people are crying out for more balance. The employer wants great performance; employees want to be happy, valued and fulfilled in their jobs, and to make an impact.

Employers used to hold all the cards, but the tide has turned. Employees are thinking about what organisations need to offer to entice them to join or stay. They are demanding flexibility. If they don't feel they're being looked after, they will migrate their talent to an employer who will provide a better balance.

The Great Resignation. Talent migration. The multi-generational workforce. Hybrid working. Remote working. The two-tiered workforce. It can feel overwhelming for employers to make the right choices and to know how to navigate this post-pandemic world as they struggle to respond to employee stress, burnout and declining mental health.

Wellbeing is the future of work. It is no longer optional. As an employer, you can't afford to take an approach that looks at just one aspect. It's not enough to offer self-care options such as a fruit bowl, a gym membership or a wellbeing app. Employers must go further if they are to ride out the waves of disruption with their workforce intact.

Employees are also expecting more of their physical environment. You need to provide brilliant workspaces that colleagues will want to return to, designed to enhance employee wellbeing. You can take this opportunity to rationalise your property portfolio to meet the needs of the hybrid working world.

Wellbeing has been treated as a perk, but during the lockdowns and isolation many of us have been thinking about what it means. It has to be integrated. You must take a holistic approach and prioritise the workforce, their workplace and their wellbeing.

Flip your current business model and create a people-centred organisation. Care for your most valuable asset. Make their wellbeing your priority. Embed a focus on wellbeing in your day-to-day operations, enrolling your leadership. Disrupt the old culture. Now is the time to focus on your people.

What is wellbeing?

Think of wellbeing holistically. It's about the whole person. For example, how they manage stress, their coping strategies, their resilience, their sleep patterns, how much they exercise, and the quality of their nutrition. Wellbeing is a virtuous circle, as outlined in the stages below:

- **Wellbeing affects health.** The better an individual's wellbeing, the healthier they tend to be. The brain and the gastrointestinal systems are closely linked. It's common to find that stress, anxiety and depression have resulted in people developing digestive issues such as IBS and stomach ulcers.

- **Health affects safety.** Do you want a fatigued pilot flying your plane? How about a distracted, stressed-out construction worker operating above you?

- **Both these things impact performance and productivity.** It all starts with wellbeing.

The wellbeing, health and safety virtuous circle

The benefits of getting it right include increased return on investment (ROI), fewer health and safety incidents, more engaged employees, higher productivity and the ability to retain talent. Your employees are happier, and so are your stakeholders. Engaged employees and a better bottom line – that's a real win-win.

Wellbeing myths

Let's look at three myths about wellbeing, debunk them and explain what you can do to overcome them.

Myth 1: We can wait to take action

It's understandable that you'd think this; many have thought it before, but this is part of the problem. The pandemic caused so much uncertainty that people stopped looking for new jobs. Vacancies fell across the board. Enter the Great Retention. We've been waiting to return to 'normal' in our journey into a post-pandemic world.

The work-from-home revolution was born. Many employees discovered a better work–life balance. Hybrid and flexible working may have begun as temporary solutions, but they became deeply rooted and are now employee expectations.

The world of work is different. In the UK, 62% say that hybrid is their preferred future way of working. It is clear that employees overwhelmingly want to hold on to that balance. The picture is similar globally – 51% of employees are working mainly or entirely remotely, with 59% saying that twelve months from now they would prefer to be still working that way.[43]

43 Bowdery, A, 'Workforce survey: Almost 20% of UK workers expect to quit in the next 12 months', PwC (24 May 2022), www.pwc.co.uk/press-room/press-releases/pwc-workforce-survey-20221.html, accessed 1 August 2022

Many organisations struggled to reimpose pre-pandemic working models. Organisations that tried to force a return to the old ways started losing their talent. Enter the Great Resignation – and it's set to stay. We now live in a world of hybrid working. Innovate, step up and engage with your people, or get left behind.

Almost one in five UK workers say that they are very or extremely likely to migrate to a new employer within the next twelve months, with millennials (those born 1981–1996) and Generation Z (1997 onward) being the employees the most likely to instigate change.

Highly skilled workers are in demand. Employees will leave if their expectations are not being met. Can you afford to be complacent and have your talent migrate to a competitor?

Myth 1 debunked. We cannot wait. If we don't act now, we risk losing our talent.

Myth 2: Wellbeing programmes do not deliver business value

This thinking used to be commonplace, but now it is out of date. Wellbeing programmes are a powerful tool, but they fail if they're not implemented and appropriately communicated. It pays to get it right the first time.

Embrace your wellbeing strategy. It needs a purpose, a framework and strong branding. Communicate it regularly and in a way that connects with a diverse workforce. In time, your strategy can make your people healthier, happier, more productive and resilient, which is reflected in reduced absenteeism and presenteeism.

The business value wellbeing can drive is considerable. A successful strategy might include the following elements:

Return on investment

- ROI is measured financially from data that is usually readily available, eg medical claims, disability and absenteeism data. Only 9% of employers currently measure the ROI of wellbeing programmes.[44] This may explain why employers are not allocating adequate budgets or resources to employee wellbeing.

- Mental health is a significant component of wellbeing. Figures for 2020–21 show that for every £1 invested in mental health interventions, there is a return of £5.30 from reduced costs associated with absenteeism, presenteeism and staff turnover.[45] Surely a 430% return on invested

---

44   Benefits and Trends Survey, 'Employers prioritised employee mental health and communications as a result of COVID-19' (Aon, 2021), www.aon.com/unitedkingdom/media-room/articles/uk-benefits-and-trends-survey-2021-covid-19, accessed 1 July 2022

45   Deloitte Mental Health and Employers, *Mental Health and Employers: The case for investment – pandemic and beyond* (2022), www2.deloitte.com/content/dam/Deloitte/uk/Documents/consultancy/deloitte-uk-mental-health-report-2022.pdf, accessed 1 July 2022

capital is appealing. This is a huge business opportunity. If you're not harnessing wellbeing, you're leaving money on the table.

Value on investment

- VOI outcomes are more difficult to measure accurately. They're intangible assets, but they significantly contribute to organisational success. They're not measured financially – they are about employee experience.

- Acquiring data for VOI requires effort and expense, such as employee engagement surveys and collecting metrics on productivity, motivation, team effectiveness and reasons for employees joining or leaving.

- In the long run, VOI is more important than ROI. Regardless of whether ROI and VOI are important to you right now, if you consider wellbeing a contributor to your bottom line, why wait to make improvements?

- Once you have an effective programme, you're unlikely to be concerned about the ROI, as the benefits come from organisational culture and productivity improvements – the VOI.

Employee value proposition

- EVP is the unique set of benefits an employee receives in return for the skills, capabilities and experience they bring to an organisation. An EVP is about defining the essence of your organisation, how it is unique and what it stands for.

- Only 28% of employees have a clear EVP. Of those that do, 85% believe it positively impacts employee engagement, and 72% believe it positively impacts retention.[46] This goes hand in hand with wellbeing.

Myth 2 debunked. Wellbeing creates value.

Myth 3: We're already doing wellbeing well

Are you really doing wellbeing well? Answer these ten questions:

1. Do you have a comprehensive wellbeing programme that is thoroughly embedded? It's worth taking time to get to know your employees and what they need to be well, stay well and perform well.

---

46   Benefits and Trends Survey, 'Employers prioritised employee mental health and communications as a result of COVID-19' (Aon, 2021), www.aon.com/unitedkingdom/media-room/articles/uk-benefits-and-trends-survey-2021-covid-19, accessed 1 July 2022

2. Are your wellbeing strategy and programme fit for purpose? One size does not fit all. Have you adapted your strategy to meet the differing needs of the five generations currently in the workforce?

3. Do you have board sponsorship for your wellbeing strategy? It is critical that wellbeing is high on the corporate agenda, with an equivalent profile to your health and safety and HR strategies.

4. Do your leaders have the right mindset? Your leaders must be developed so they can believe in, model and live this new way of thinking.

5. Do you involve your workforce and other stakeholders in your wellbeing programme offering? Do you know what they want? Almost a third of employers do not consult with their employees to understand their needs.[47]

6. Do you have a two-tiered workforce? We now have some employees who can take advantage of hybrid or remote working, which improves their wellbeing. What about the 45% of workers who have to go to an office, a hospital or a restaurant every day?[48] They may have had to go into their

---

47   Benefits and Trends Survey, 'Employers prioritised employee mental health and communications as a result of COVID-19' (Aon, 2021), www.aon.com/unitedkingdom/media-room/articles/uk-benefits-and-trends-survey-2021-covid-19, accessed 1 July 2022

48   PwC, 'Global Workforce Hopes and Fears Survey 2022' (24 May 2022), www.pwc.com/gx/en/issues/workforce/hopes-and-fears-2022.html accessed 1 August 2022

physical workplace every day of the pandemic. These cohorts might require different wellbeing support.

7. Do you have a strategy to support the wellbeing of those who permanently work remotely? Human connections are vital. We are social creatures. It's important to factor in loneliness and mental health challenges stemming from isolation.

8. Do you have a comprehensive communications and engagement plan to promote and embed wellbeing? You must take *all* your people along with you. You can't pay lip service to this. Thinking that just some of you can buy into this philosophy is a mistake. Culture change involves everyone.

9. Do you say, 'We have an employee assistance programme that employees can contact if they have an issue'? That is not enough. Only 6% of employees use this programme each year.[49] You've got to do more. Your competitors are doing more – 77% of employers have a formalised health and wellbeing strategy or will within the next twelve to eighteen months.[50]

---

49   Deloitte Mental Health and Employers, *Mental Health and Employers: The case for investment – pandemic and beyond* (2022), www2.deloitte.com/content/dam/Deloitte/uk/Documents/consultancy/deloitte-uk-mental-health-report-2022.pdf, accessed 1 July 2022

50   Benefits and Trends Survey, 'Employers prioritised employee mental health and communications as a result of COVID-19' (Aon, 2021), www.aon.com/unitedkingdom/media-room/articles/uk-benefits-and-trends-survey-2021-covid-19, accessed 1 July 2022

10. Where does accountability and governance for wellbeing sit in your organisation? Wellbeing, health and safety are covered under your duty of care as an employer and touch all parts of your organisation. Ownership and accountability are often fragmented. Embedding the right wellbeing, health and safety culture is the responsibility of all. Modern organisations should be integrating their wellbeing, health and safety services so that governance, accountability and day-to-day operations are clear.

Myth 3 debunked: If you've answered no to any of these questions, you must reconsider your wellbeing strategy and programmes.

Your wellbeing, health and safety strategies are paramount to success. Overcoming the three myths I have described will serve your organisation for many years to come. You are a disruptor, and you need to act. You can create lasting business value by investing in wellbeing.

Sarah Piddington was born in Sydney and has been London-based since 2002. She has been an expert consultant in health and safety, wellbeing and mental health for twenty years.

Through her W3 Programme (Wellbeing, Workforce and Workplace), she advises directors on how to adapt to the changing world and respond to modern workforce challenges, including mental health and the future of work.

Sarah is a trusted advisor who is passionate about future-proofing organisations by putting wellbeing, health and safety at the heart of their business in a post-Covid-19 world.

Sarah has worked with 100+ corporate and public sector organisations, supporting them in creating an engaged workforce by implementing strategies to help their people thrive. Organisations include BT, Citi, McKinsey & Company, British Transport Police and Overbury.

🌐 safeandwelltogether.com

in www.linkedin.com/in/sarahpiddington

CHAPTER 12

Disruptors – Political, Economic, Social And Technological

ANTHONY POLLOCK

The last two centuries have been characterised by continual technological disruption, and the rate of change continues to increase as we move from Web 2.0 to Web 5.0. This creates divisions between those brought up on the new technology and those who are older. My children do not remember a world before mobile phones, email and the internet. To them, red telephone boxes are a museum piece from the dim and distant past. I travelled on steam trains and started work before the invention of the personal computer, in a time when accountancy was completely manual and calculators were considered so dangerously modern that we were banned from using them during our training contract, since adding up was a crucial skill. The PC and spreadsheets completely changed this practice within six years.

Technological disruption started with the application of technology to agricultural production. In the eighteenth century, the seed drill and various other new types of equipment transformed agricultural production, and this supported a growth in population throughout the nineteenth century. Manufacturing was transformed by new inventions such as the spinning jenny, which irrevocably changed the clothing industry – handloom weavers being a major casualty of industrialisation. The development of canals, railways and the steam ship transformed the distribution of raw materials and finished products. Wood was replaced by coal, and later oil and gas, as fuel to power industry and commerce. Even the nation's diet changed with the ability to transport fresh food into cities such as London.

In the last fifty years, the development of electronics and its application to radio, television, telecommunications and computing has transformed our society and our working life. This has led to a complete evolution in the world of work in terms of our efficiency, experience and opportunity. Disruption has not only changed business practices; it has also completely changed the job market. Some jobs, such as typists, have completely disappeared and new jobs such as word processors, IT consultants and digital marketers have been created that no one even imagined in 1976.

Disruption caused by war and revolution

Alongside commercially driven technological change, war and military conflict have increased the pace of disruptive change. The First World War led to the accelerated development of aircraft, motorised transport, machine guns and heavy artillery. Government organisations focusing on winning the war transformed society, increasing the level of government direction and control.

In the interwar years, with the development of new industries, new companies such as Rolls-Royce, the de Havilland Aircraft Company, the Bristol Aeroplane Company, and Vickers prospered. The Second World War accelerated the development of electronic applications such as wireless, radar and computing.

The Cold War required further accelerated development to keep ahead of the Russians. This continued the disruptive process, out of which came further computer development and the miniaturisation of electronics. The internet was invented to provide communication in a post-nuclear-war society, following the destruction of the main command and control centres. The internet was then further developed following the invention of the PC and the expansion of PC networks, first within offices and then on a wider basis, culminating in their connection to the web.

Today, the computer revolution and the web have moved on to the development of cloud computing and fuelled what we call 'globalisation'. Without this connectivity it would have been impossible to create large global companies with the ability to command and control from head offices in the USA, the UK, Japan or the EU.

The Russian revolutions in 1905 and 1917, together with the revolutions in China in 1911 and 1949, disrupted the social, economic and political fabric of those countries and influenced attitudes around the world. These events changed the expectations of countries outside Europe, giving hope to those who had been colonised by the Western Powers in the nineteenth century that it was possible to overthrow their colonial rulers and run their own affairs.

The development of supranational governments

The Treaty of Versailles in 1919–20 disrupted the pre-war settlement based on the 1815 Treaty of Vienna and led to the development of supranational governments. The formation of the League of Nations was the first attempt to regulate such relations. Western democracies who had lost many men during WW1 were keen to develop alternatives to war as a resolution to international conflict. This experiment failed following Italy's invasion of Abyssinia in 1935 and the German takeover of Austria in 1938, and Czechoslovakia in 1938/9. The league had no power, except moral authority, to compel nation states to stop short of war and so this proved unsuccessful.

The experience of successfully winning the war by using policies of social and economic command and control influenced post-WW1 political structures and organisation, especially in Russia, Germany, Italy and Spain. The supposed success of the five-year economic plans following the Wall Street stock market crash in 1929 provided an alternative model to the traditional free market capitalism. The departure of national currencies from linkage to the price of gold freed governments to change their economic policies.

The publication of *The General Theory of Employment, Interest and Money* by John Maynard-Keynes[51] transformed the intellectual climate in the field of economics. Keynes' analysis allowed national governments to use his theory to develop macroeconomic policy which placed governments themselves at the heart of economic and social policy, promising full employment and social progress. Governments tried to reconcile the

---

51   Keynes, JM, *The General Theory of Employment, Interest and Money* (CreateSpace Independent Publishing Platform, 2013)

competing demands of industry and workers through the application of debt-financed government spending. The consequence of this was to bake in initially low levels of annual inflation. The effect of inflation in the 1950s and early 1960s was mitigated by the existence of sufficient worldwide demand for products from the USA and UK. By the mid-1960s, the European production facilities had revived sufficiently behind EEC tariff walls to provide increased competition in world markets and inflation started to rise above the previously low levels, which disrupted the delicate balance between the various parties in society.

The 1970s saw further disruption through inflation. Governments increased the money supply according to Keynesian theory, but the problem of greater competition between workers and industry to keep ahead of the inflationary spiral made management of the economy more difficult. The rises in raw material costs for oil – a 300% increase in 1973 – and raw materials from newly independent countries around the world further fuelled inflation in Western countries. The failure of the Keynesian theory by the end of the 1970s caused the development of a new economic theory in the 1980s called 'monetarism' which is forever associated with Mrs Thatcher. This has since held sway in the UK.

What of the future? What are the current trends and how do we navigate any harmful application of technological, political and governmental disruption?

Who do governments serve?

What is the future relationship between governments and the people? In the UK and much of the Western world we have rejected the divine right of kings over the last 300 years and adopted an approach where the government is seen as a servant of the people. In theory, government only intervenes when it must and lets the populace get on with their lives the rest of the time. In the twenty-first century the role of government has expanded to include pursuing a relentless intrusion through new laws and regulations and claiming that these are for our benefit. This has developed to such an extent that instead of everything being legal unless it is specifically illegal, we face the opposite. We now need to obtain official permission for many things that we do. Are governments and their associated bureaucracies up to the task of managing these complexities? Can they anticipate the unforeseen consequences of their decisions and the way these intervene in our lives? I am convinced the answer is no.

Technocratic totalitarianism

In China we see the next step in this new top-down increase in government control in the way it is developing the use of face recognition and social credit systems to provide an even stronger level of social control over its population. I read a report by a visitor to China who had to use his mobile phone to hire a bicycle. The phone was connected to his bank account and his government computer file. At first glance this seems efficient in that the government knows where the bicycle is, it encourages its use and no one can steal it. However, if your political views are deviant then you will not be able to hire the bicycle, you may have to pay more for it or, if your account is not in credit, you may not be able to hire the bicycle to go to work at all. This is obviously designed to control the attitudes and behaviours of the population. Could this system be coming to the West? Fortunately, we don't currently have internet systems reliable enough to provide this level of control.

The end of the rules-based international order?

The development of the UN in the post-1945 period and its associated agencies has created a framework of intergovernmental cooperation based around the expectation of creating global good arising from the rules-based international economic order. This provides a better framework for resolving differences than national warmongering. It has been largely successful in preventing large-scale conflict since 1945, but the organisation is increasingly reaching into areas of national concern. Various global warming climate summits since 2000 have resulted in government policy being made in conformity with the recommendations adopted by these bodies. In the UK we have seen repeated policy directives, starting with Agenda 21 and currently being reflected in the policy of net zero. Governments are proclaiming their commitment to green credentials by bringing forward legislation to achieve net zero by 2035.

This policy is disruptive to our current economic model. Our capacity to generate electricity cannot meet the needs of net zero, and its expansion to meet future needs will take over ten years. We have seen increases in renewable energy such as solar and wind but this is not available 24/7, 365 days a year and therefore requires either significant hydropower capacity or new conventional power stations. The shift of current hydrocarbon energy usage for transport, domestic heating and commercial purposes to the electricity grid has not been fully calculated, planned or funded so its achievability must be in doubt.

We could be facing a world where lateness excuses change from 'leaves on the railway line' or 'motorway congestion' to 'my car battery could not be charged overnight' or 'my train wouldn't run because there wasn't enough electricity capacity'. How are we going to live if we can't charge our electronic devices because there isn't enough capacity? Do we depend too much on unreliable renewables? Germany is currently experiencing a major challenge due to its reliance on Russian gas and oil supplies, notwithstanding its substantial achievement in developing a large amount of wind and solar capacity. The disruption of global regulation is having a major impact on the daily lives of ordinary people. Will these people continue to be as committed to the green revolution when they understand the true financial and social cost to them, their families and their communities?

Economic, technological, social and political disruption is here to stay. These changes will not slow down. They are of themselves morally neutral. It is those applying the technology who are the moral, immoral or amoral actors. We must remain vigilant and engaged with the impact of the changes and disruptions that are happening around us. We must avoid being the proverbial frog in the pan of boiling water and must be prepared to take appropriate action and not just accept what is handed down to us from on high.

Anthony Pollock has been a chartered accountant for over thirty-five years, spending fifteen years working for professional public practices, fifteen years running his own sole practice, and over ten years as a CFO assisting start-ups and early-stage businesses. Knowledgeable, personable, intelligent and hands-on, Anthony enjoys helping successful business owners to achieve their objectives.

For twenty-five years Anthony has worked in his spare time as an elected borough councillor on Wokingham Borough Council, a unitary authority. His responsibilities include finance, setting up the new local education authority within eleven months, highways, and adult social care.

🌐   https://anthonypollock.co.uk

in   www.linkedin.com/in/anthony-pollock-virtual-cfo-services

CHAPTER 13

The Customer Is Not *Always* Right: Disrupting Customers In Complex Sales Environments

TIM ROBERTSON

You have probably heard of the phrase 'the customer is always right', which has been firmly engrained in the minds of customer service representatives for a couple of decades. In B2B selling environments, this old adage is not always the case.

The internet has changed the way we do business. Customers are becoming savvier and understand solutions much better because of the availability of information but, like the common practice of patient self-diagnosis, often customers are self-diagnosing problems with the wrong solutions.

Finding and satisfying customer needs has long been the tenet of most solution sales experts, but customers are not always right when it comes to their recognised and unrecognised needs. Customers often do not know what they want until they see it, and even then there are many instances when they cannot identify what they really need until after they have purchased something else. The benefits of hindsight. Recent evidence suggests that to be effective in B2B sales you have to disrupt the customer's thinking and show them a new set of needs.[52]

An experienced and successful salesperson will tell you that relationships are the key to any sale – and that trying to challenge or teach the customer is likely to lead to reactance and defensiveness – but in 2012 the world of sales was astounded by the work of two authors, Dixon and Adamson, who wrote a revolutionary book called *The Challenger Sale*.[53] The authors suggested that the

52   Hohenschwert, L, and Geiger, S, 'Interpersonal influence strategies in complex B2B sales and the socio-cognitive construction of relationship value', *Industrial Marketing Management*, Volume 49 (August 2015), 139–150, https://doi.org/10.1016/j.indmarman.2015.05.027, accessed 4 August 2022

53   Dixon, M, and Adamson, B, *The Challenger Sale: How to take control of the customer conversation* (Portfolio Penguin, 2013)

most successful salespeople were those who challenged the customer and their thinking. The book caused a massive reaction by claiming that solution selling and relationships were dead, and the new era was for the so-called 'challenger' salesperson to teach the customer what they really needed.

The fiercest competition on any B2B sale is not the other company, waiting in the wings to scoop down and take the deal away from the salesperson, it's the customer themself. According to research, up to 60% of deals stall because of one factor: status quo bias.[54]

Status quo bias

Researchers Richard Zeckhauser and William Samuelson first introduced the term 'status quo bias' in 1988.[55] They define it as, 'A tendency to be overly concerned with what exists at present and a failure to adequately consider alternative courses of action.' In other words, we are afraid of change because it might disrupt what we already have, and tend to stick with the current choice or decision even if it's not providing any benefits. This is also known as 'the devil you know', since it can be hard for

---

54   Dixon, M, and McKenna, T, 'Stop Losing Sales to Customer Indecision', *Harvard Business Review* (24 June 2022), https://hbr.org/2022/06/stop-losing-sales-to-customer-indecision, accessed 4 August 2022

55   Samuelson, W, and Zeckhauser, R, 'Status Quo Bias in Decision Making', *Journal of Risk and Uncertainty*, Volume 1, No 1 (March 1988), pp 7-59, https://scholar.harvard.edu/files/rzeckhauser/files/status_quo_bias_in_decision_making.pdf, accessed 6 July 2022

people to change a situation they know is undesirable but is nonetheless familiar. This reluctance can affect their behaviours and decisions and they often perceive changes as detriments or losses.

The status quo bias also significantly affects our purchasing decisions. Overcoming it can sway customers to purchase a new product or service with you, and reinforcing this bias can make them remain loyal to your brand as one they are familiar with.

In his book, *Why We Buy*,[56] Paco Underhill suggests that, 'We tend to hold things more dear to us after we buy them.' This is sometimes called 'the endowment effect' – people apply more value to something they already own than they would if they didn't own it. A similar situation occurs in a project where monies have already been spent on a particular solution, sometimes called 'the sunk cost fallacy', when people think something along the lines of 'We've spent this money already; we can't waste it.' We all have our biases.

According to researchers such as Daniel Kahneman and Amos Tversky, we're hardwired to make decisions in ways that seem logical but are actually completely irrational.[57] We tend to focus on what's in front of us rather than

---

56   Underhill, P, *Why We Buy: The science of shopping* (Simon & Schuster, 2008)

57   Tversky, A, and Kahneman, D, 'Loss Aversion in Riskless Choice: A Reference-Dependent Model', in Kahneman, D, and Tversky, A, (Eds), 'Choices, Values, and Frames' (Cambridge University Press, 2000), https://doi.org/10.1017/CBO9780511803475.008, accessed 4 August 2022

looking at the big picture, and we make assumptions based on our own experiences that don't apply to everyone else. In both cases, it's easy to see how these biases might lead us astray when making decisions about where to invest our resources next.

Underhill also suggests the following thoughts go through people's minds: 'There's no danger in staying put, I don't want to risk a bad outcome in my next decision.' This can be overridden by new information and can lead to people changing their minds, but it still influences our decision-making process.

Neuroscientists have found that the amygdala, which is the centre for our danger response of fight, flight or freeze, has a strong preference for stability. We don't want to endanger ourselves by deciding on something that's different from the status quo.

In other words, we're good at keeping things the same. This can be a real problem for businesses who are trying to innovate and grow but are unsure about what direction they should go in next, or where they should focus their efforts.

How to overcome status quo bias in the sales process

So, what's the answer? In essence, the authors of *The Challenger Sale* were right, but it is actually *how* this is done rather than *what* is done that makes all the difference.

Overcoming the status quo bias requires you to show potential customers how your products or services can meet any unconsidered needs they may have. An unconsidered or unrecognised need is a need that the customer has not considered as being as important as we are suggesting it is. I will use an example from my own experience to illustrate this point.

A few months back, I had a problem. I noticed that one of my tyres was losing tread. It couldn't be repaired or replaced, so I took my car down to the local garage to get it fixed. I told the guy at the front desk that I needed a new tyre, and he said 'No problem', and started taking my car on the ramp to replace it. But five minutes later, he came back out and said: 'Sorry – you're going to need four new tyres.'

He showed me how much tread was left on each tyre – and how much more would be lost if we didn't replace them all now. He also explained that if I only let him replace one, it would be on his conscience if I were stopped by the police and got three points on my licence for each tyre (as well as a fine of £300 per tyre). That would lead to me being disqualified for six months – and still needing four new tyres.

I knew there were laws against driving with bald tyres, but this made me realise how serious it could be if you got caught. It wasn't just something nice-to-have; it was a need-to-have and the mechanic raised the importance of this to me.

So how do we do this?

The first thing you need to do is highlight the unrecognised needs that your customers have, show them how their current situation will put them in more difficulties or risk if they stay as they are, and explain that they will have a greater chance of reaching their goals if they embrace change.

Then, highlight your strengths and show them how your product or service will meet their unconsidered needs and resolve their risks. When it comes to sales, the best salespeople are those who can challenge their customers' assumptions *without offending them*.

Challenging can often cause both the salesperson and the customer to grow further apart rather than closer. In some cases, you may even come across as arrogant or condescending. Not everyone wants to be 'taught' without having asked for it. Not every customer wants to feel like they're being schooled by a know-it-all; some people just want someone who understands them and what they're going through, which is where empathetic reframing comes in.

By showing empathy for your customer's position and then showing them an alternative view through storytelling about another customer similar to them, you can help change their perspective without making them feel like they've been called out for having made an error of judgement.

But you need to get their attention – and fast.

The main way you can do this is by introducing unconsidered needs that exist beyond your prospect's obvious stated needs. This means finding needs that are not currently part of their thinking – unconsidered, unmet or underappreciated gaps and opportunities within their business.

These can be experiences that you have had with previous customers that have led to them making bad choices and ending up in risky situations. You need to tell stories of these experiences in a way that highlights what the previous customer's situation was, what decisions they made and what the eventual risky outcome was.

The magic of storytelling

Storytelling is one of the most powerful tools in business. It can help you connect with your audience and get them to feel something – whether that feeling is positive or negative. You don't have to be a writer or an expert storyteller to benefit from storytelling. You just need to understand how it works, and then apply it to your business.

There are two things that happen when you share a story: emotional connection and context connection.

Emotional connection happens first – the reader feels something, whether that's anger or joy, happiness or sadness. Then comes logical connection – the reader starts to think about what they've just read in terms of their own life and how it might be applicable to them.

Context connection is when your customer adds context to what you're sharing. If you're just sharing facts and figures, your audience member doesn't know in what scene you are setting these figures. They don't know the background or origin of where they come from. They don't know whether these are good figures in the face of adversity or poor figures in the face of an easy time.

This is because stories have a way of connecting with our emotions in a way that is more powerful than just plain facts or figures can ever be. That's why, when you go into a film theatre and sit down, it doesn't take long before everyone starts sniffling and blowing their noses because of all those sad moments in the movie.

As a next step, you align your solution's specific strengths with the unrecognised needs you have just introduced. This creates a sense of urgency and importance that can compel your prospect to change.

This meeting point between your prospect's unrecognised needs and the specific strengths your solution offers is where you can establish that your company is uniquely positioned to drive a better, more valuable future situation. Now your customer has a reason to believe and care about your strengths and capabilities, which go from not adding value to being utterly invaluable.

One last word: if you're trying to keep a customer, the situation is reversed. In B2B sales, we are often trying to retain existing large accounts and the status quo bias often needs to be reinforced to stay with you. If you are trying to persuade existing customers to renew or expand their relationship with you, you need to reinforce the emotional aspects of their relationship with your services and make change seem safe as long as it's with you.

Tim Robertson is a B2B sales performance specialist. A widely respected consultant, he is generally considered to be a leading authority on the subject. He is passionate about sales success in the B2B environment using the latest decision-making science methods.

With a background in science, Tim's career in business and senior management spans thirty years, during which time he has been a top-performing director and established and run courses on leadership within many varied business sectors. He is currently undertaking a doctorate, researching novel ways of using video conferencing to sell effectively.

Tim has worked across many sectors globally with clients large and small – from two-man start-ups to international conglomerates with household names – and has a flexible, approachable style.

in www.linkedin.com/in/timrobertsoninsight

CHAPTER 14

Care Is Key

MALCOLM TULLETT

Do you care about people, places, things or activities and I mean, *really* care? My social media strapline is 'Passionate about your safety – and that's not achieved by accident', so when I was approached to collaborate on this book I thought, 'What better place to start?' For me, being passionate is all about caring. It's easy to disrupt things too, especially when you don't care, but that's tantamount to vandalism, isn't it?

All sectors of our life, whether this be family, friends, leisure, our environment or work, are constantly changing – disruption is normal. At first glance, the word conjures up negative thoughts of disturbance, disorder or problem-making (eg disruption to travel plans etc), but it also has a positive connotation when used to mean to interrupt or break away from the normal course of action or accepted custom and practice (eg disruption to the expensive encyclopaedia market by the free and easy-to-access Wikipedia platform).

The difference, for me, is the care, or passion, of the individual(s) doing the disrupting for the issue at hand. My passion is all about care and I have routinely and regularly disrupted my own occupational safety and health (OSH) industry by insisting that the widely accepted 'legal' term 'duty of care' is, de facto, an oxymoron, as there is no need to impose a duty to care on someone who truly cares.

So, just care.

As a trustee of one of my professional bodies, some years ago now, I was directed to a newspaper article that highlighted the practical but inappropriate application of the oxymoron, where a head teacher had banned conker (horse chestnut) fights, a very English childhood playground pastime. On further investigation, it transpired that s/he had misunderstood the basis of both 'reasonable' OSH standards and the 'duty' of care. I just couldn't help myself. I arranged for the head teacher to be informed that there was no likelihood of any 'significant' injury, other than hurt pride when losing a champion conker, and even if anyone sustained any form of injury, it was probably going to be no more than a bruised knuckle. The response was swift and, again, the newspaper got wind of it: the concern was a piece of conker shrapnel entering the eye. The gauntlet had been laid and low and behold my fellow trustees accepted the challenge and staged the first World Conker Championship. We (the safety professionals) entered a team and our uniform included heavy-duty protective clothing, in the heat of summer I might add, boxing head gear, with safety goggles and boxing gloves. The press loved it. It made front page news and the point was made.

This head teacher obviously cared but took the 'duty' of care too far. S/he was disrupting the age-old activity, that had never given rise to a significant injury, but for the wrong reasons, although I do understand that care for others and self-protection, through the fear of a liability claim in this instance, are not mutually exclusive. In fact, true disruption is in itself a risky business and there is no guarantee that any new disruptive innovation will gain a foothold in an industry or practice, and many people simply keep quiet for fear of being seen as a disruptor. Often, to keep quiet, although maintaining the status quo and calm, risks inactivity and stagnation, so be prepared; you'll be damned if you do and damned if you don't.

So, take up the challenge.

I've been called many things in my life and among those that are repeatable is being an amiable maverick. I have always been a risk-taker but have never sought to cause pain or unnecessary disturbance, but instead to challenge inappropriate rules and potentially dangerous customs and practices while driving radical change, not as an idealist but to secure improvements, for all. As an example, way back in the early 1990s I was the station commander at Euston Fire Station, in London, and became frustrated (*vis-à-vis* passionate) at not being able to arrange for station administration to be undertaken by a non-uniformed member of staff. The routine response was always, 'It's not done that way in the fire service,' and even with being considered an unconventional oddball, I persisted in my quest until I was called in for a 'fireside chat' with the area commander. Without any niceties, 'You're far too entrepreneurial for the fire service' was the opening line, and it deteriorated from there. Being promoted into a position in headquarters didn't shut me up.

So, be assertive.

Ironically for the fire service, I was seconded to an outsourced transformation team on the basis that I was both a problem-solver and original thinker, probably now referred to as a thought leader. The team was charged with streamlining management processes, as part of an overriding change management strategy, which followed on the back of the findings of a report into a double firefighter fatality, at a serious fire in the East End of London. Strangely enough, I had also been a member of the incident investigation team and had direct knowledge and experience of the findings. During my period of secondment, the opportunity arose to revisit my entrepreneurial view of life as a station commander and I suggested that these essentially operational officers were being bogged down with routine administration that was taking their eye off the ball. Low and behold, the recommendation was made by the external consultants that an administration budget be provided to stations, for the commander to use for administrative support – so not that entrepreneurial after all and in London, at least, my disruptive thinking gave rise to enhanced efficiency and effectiveness, for the benefit of firefighter safety. Not that it was sold that way.

So, be tenacious.

Since leaving the fire service, I have been either a freelance fire and safety practitioner or, since the late 1990s, run my own fire and consultancy business – gamekeeper turned poacher. Some might say that's all about being disruptive and they may well be right; I saw my role as understanding that there are always at least three ways of looking at an issue, particularly when it comes to interpreting guidance.

As a fire safety inspecting officer and, subsequently, a team leader and policy officer, I was able to look at all sides of the issue and seek both a consensus and a 'reasonable' solution that achieved the 'functional' requirements. To this day, I find myself discussing various options quite passionately with those of fixed views. Take, for instance, the legislative response to the Grenfell fire tragedy, where so many, both inside and outside of the fire and safety industry, look at just the emotional solutions, without any thought about how these solutions are to be put into effect.

So, be forthright.

There have been numerous occasions when I have argued the complete reverse of the 'common sense' of the crowd, simply because their suggestions seem to be based on what sounds right, emotionally, at the time. It is a bit unnerving when the pack turn on me, simply because I just might be in a minority of one but correct. It is so important that, if I do get proved wrong, I accept the opposing opinion and carry on with the discussion, without spitting out my dummy.

So, be pragmatic.

What about my own business? I'd like to think I've been a positive disruptor there too as, fortunately, I have always managed to maintain a great team. We all have different leadership styles but I have always insisted that members of my team tell me what I should hear, not what they think I want to hear.

Not only am I a disruptor by nature, but I go out of my way to encourage others to do the same. I can't see the point in not being inquisitive and challenging the status quo. There is of course a time and place for everything, so

I revert to my early leadership training when I was taught the John Adair model of task, team and individual needs. This simple and highly practical framework provided a whole range of strategies for overcoming complex management challenges.

In essence, the task needs are met by the team, which has needs of its own but the team comprises individuals, who all have the ability to lead, follow and/or be creative, depending on the working environment. For me, that environment has always needed to encourage robust and innovative outcomes and this can only ever come about following an open and honest dialogue. As soon as one of the team, who might just be holding that golden nugget of disruption, feels constrained by the fear of getting it wrong, there'll be no creativity.

So, be challenging.

As I said in opening, my passion is care. I never constrain any individual to keep quiet, even if they want to challenge the status quo or to be revolutionary, as that's how great ideas are born. In our office, we have an oft-repeated mantra that says, 'I trust you to make mistakes.' Without that safety net, none of the team would ever feel safe to think differently.

Sometimes it's just a feeling, and even then the team are encouraged to be open and honest, with a view to driving them all towards that light-bulb moment – the disruptive thinking that all of us need.

So, trust your gut and those of your team.

In the family setting, when one person speaks candidly, as long as it is based on love and care for the others the family will accept it, even when it hurts. In loving families, the idea of collective support brings with it the love and care needed to say it as it is, which is a bit like a military or fire service debrief. I have been fortunate to be involved in many a debrief where, though brutal, the only expectation is to learn from mistakes.

In these environments, disruption is the norm and system/ process change is constant. I have also been involved in corporate mastermind sessions where issues are pulled apart, to rebuild better.

So, be cruel to be kind.

This idea of family support has been a constant motivator for me in all of the various communities in which I am involved – whether it be home, my network of friends and acquaintances, leisure or work – as love and affection are the basis of care and without them, we are lost.

The workplace, for instance, is also a family environment, especially as most of you reading this will be spending more time at work than you do at leisure, unless of course you do not work, for whatever reason, or you are wealthy enough not to, in your own right.

As such, isn't it about time that all business leaders understand that the wellbeing of their staff, both as individuals and collectively, is the essence of a happy team? Happy teams are more creative, more efficient and effective and, as a result, more productive.

Without even thinking about 'statutory compliance' or having to tick any of the 'duty of care' boxes, I have been paid back in bucketloads when a member of staff has needed help and I have given it, with love. It might be an advance in wages, it might be time off at short notice or even unpaid leave, or something as simple as having a chat or saying thank you, but that simple gesture of support helps them to feel valuable and cherished.

What more could you ever want?

So, be kind.

Malcolm Tullett has an insider's view of risk and safety. Having served as a senior operational fire officer in the London Fire Brigade, he has seen fatalities first-hand and played a pivotal role in clearing up the mess when things go wrong. Now, as a business owner advising all types of organisations from small to blue-chip on health and safety matters, he understands the challenges of protecting the wellbeing and safety of staff and property.

Before becoming a firefighter, Malcolm attended naval college, which is where his interest in and understanding of risk and safety developed. At sea, he continued to learn and analyse the rationale and effectiveness of long-standing practices, always questioning processes that didn't work – a habit that has continued throughout his career and life.

🌐 malcolmtullett.com

💼 www.linkedin.com/in/malcolmtullett

🐦 @malcolmtullett

CHAPTER 15

The Three Keys To Unlocking Your Disruptive Potential

JANE YOUNG

'Life is a game, play it.'
– Mother Teresa[58]

For two decades, I've been fascinated by the world of work. Morbid curiosity may be a more accurate description, a bit like the cultural fascination we have

---

58   Ceban, Galina, 'Passion for Life!', *Forum*, Volume 41, No 3 (July 2003), p48

with natural disasters, serial killers and car crashes. Many philosophers and psychologists believe we find nasty things compelling because it's useful to be hyper-aware of dangers that threaten our survival. Others believe that we all yearn to experience other people's suffering because it helps us develop empathy and strengthen social bonds.

Whether I yearn to experience the suffering of people who spend their lives in a job that's devoid of meaning, or can't resist the allure of bizarre leadership behaviours and legacy structures that threaten our survival, I have always been intrigued by the fact so many of us have accepted the modus operandi of the ordinary world of work for so long.

Up until now, that is.

The power balance has shifted from employer to employee. A new world of work is emerging, as record numbers of people quit their jobs amid the 'Great Resignation'. Perhaps the 'Great Aspiration' is a better term to describe the search for meaning, fulfilment and growth that's leading to vast swathes of the population craving more than a pay cheque.

The pandemic may have accelerated this search for meaning, but a generational tidal wave has been gathering pace for years.

The humanisation of work has begun and disruptors hold the keys to a better world: a world that balances people, planet and profit; a world that doesn't grind its people down and burn them out, but lifts them up.

An alternative future

Disruptors have transformational superpowers, and with these powers comes great responsibility. If we can positively disrupt the way we live, work and get things done, the future no longer looms as some scary, apocalyptic place. Instead, it's a place that doesn't yet exist, that disruptors must create.

Disruptors' greatest creativity is ignited by crisis. Crisis presents an opportunity to dip into the reservoirs of our humanity; to bring about profound changes in society by rising to new levels of strength and conviction that we didn't know we possessed, as we each become the disruptor that we were meant to be.

To take on this challenge, disruptors have a responsibility to tell stories and paint pictures of an alternative future. A future that offers something beyond the sticky froth of conventional wisdom. A future that lifts people out of the distracting traps of status anxiety, fear of failure, lack of trust, worthlessness, performance paranoia and loneliness, so we're free to apply our energy and focus to the real work: the work of positive disruption.

At their core, disruptors create meaning. Through their visions of a better future, strategic clarity and proficiency in difficult things, they change the way people think, feel and act; and change the way work gets done.

To take responsibility for fulfilling our disruptor's destiny is to pick up the heaviest burden we can bear and carry it up the highest mountain, one small step at a time. It's from this effort that meaning emerges, making the suffering in life worthwhile. Such is the hero's journey that underpins Hollywood movies and bestsellers: the greater the sacrifice, the more heroic we become.

Disruptors aren't immune to guilt, shame, regret, lack of discipline, bad habits, procrastination, arrogance, resentment, or any other intrusion that wrenches humans further apart from who they could be. It's the act of striving to discard these pernicious ways and close this gap that characterises the journey from current reality and its broken systems to the better, brighter future we're called to create.

German Philosopher Martin Heidegger (1889–1976) described individual human existences as being *geworfen*, or 'thrown', into the world.[59] There's nothing we can do about this: we're each assigned a random character and circumstances when we're born into the game of life.

What we do with this character – which games we choose to play or create, which burden we lift, which hill we climb

---

59   Wrathall, MA, *The Cambridge Heidegger Lexicon* (Cambridge University Press, 3 January 2021)

and what and whom we take responsibility for along the way – is up for grabs. The disruptor's game is one of positive change, but the distinct purpose(s) you pursue are up to you.

The world needs some work. It is crying out for visionaries and change-makers to step into the arena and summon the forces of disruption to create a better world. The journey begins internally, with the creation of a better self. Are you ready?

The first key: stop looking for your purpose

'He who has a why can bear any how.'
– Friedrich Nietzsche[60]

Humans have a deep instinct for meaning. Purpose matters. A study of 7,000 people across all walks of life found that people who lack a strong life purpose – defined as 'a self-organising life aim that stimulates goals' – are more likely to die early than those who don't.[61] The researchers were shocked to discover that purpose is more important for decreasing risk of death than avoiding drinking and smoking or getting regular exercise. 'Just like

---

60   Nietzsche, F, *Twilight of the Idols or How to Philosophize with a Hammer* [Kindle edition of new translation by Daniel Fidel Ferrer] (Kuhn von Verden, 23 February 2021)

61   Alimujiang, A, Wiensch, A, Boss, J, et al, 'Association Between Life Purpose and Mortality Among US Adults Older Than 50 Years', *JAMA Netw Open* (2019;2(5):e194270), https://jamanetwork.com/journals/jamanetworkopen/fullarticle/2734064, accessed 28 July 2022

people have basic physical needs, like to sleep and eat and drink, they have basic psychological needs,' says professor Alan Rozanski.[62] 'The need for meaning and purpose is number one. It's the deepest driver of wellbeing there is.'

On a personal level, the search for purpose brings existential angst to many a disruptor. If you have a single, defined, lifelong purpose, congratulations – you're a rare breed. For most of us, the search for an answer to the question 'How do I find my purpose?' induces a tortuous tailspin that depletes our energy, and culminates in endless false starts that erode self-belief and hamper the realisation of our disruptive potential. In truth, you don't *find* your purpose, you *build* it. You develop it, by doing the work.

Most of us don't have a sole purpose – we have multiple sources of purpose that span work, family and community; and purpose is seldom static: it shifts over time, as our lives evolve through stages of maturity. That's why focusing on action is more fruitful for disruptors than waiting for a divine calling to poke us in the face before we act, or fixating on the crafting of an elegant one-liner that encapsules our perpetual 'Why?'

Some things we spend time on matter, others don't. The act of doing something worthwhile develops our sense

---

62   Gordon, M, 'What's Your Purpose? Finding A Sense Of Meaning In Life Is Linked to Health', NPR (25 May 2019), www.npr.org/sections/health-shots/2019/05/25/726695968/whats-your-purpose-finding-a-sense-of-meaning-in-life-is-linked-to-health, accessed 28 July 2022

of purpose. Pick from a long list of possible good things, make a bad plan (it will change), do, learn and adapt… and meaning grows.

Don't sweat your bliss. Researchers from Columbia University found that people who believe pursuing passion means following what brings them joy are less likely to succeed than those who believe that it's about focusing on what you care about.[63] Passion wanes, while caring powers persistence.

The second key: craft a bold and epic tale of disruption

Disruptors are visionaries: they see things that others don't. As agents of change, we need others to see what we see too.

Most change efforts fizzle and die. According to McKinsey, 70% of change initiatives fall short; and Patrick Hoverstadt, in his book *The Fractal Organization*,[64] claims that a whopping 90–98% of strategy is never implemented.

How do you succeed, against all odds, in departing the ordinary world, slaying the dragon and returning to your village with the elixir?

---

63   Jachimowicz, J, 'The Dynamic Nature of Passion: Understanding the Pursuit, Experience, and Perception of Passion', Columbia University Libraries (12 April 2019), https://academiccommons.columbia.edu/doi/10.7916/d8-df1p-ev15, accessed 28 July 2022

64   Hoverstadt, P, *The Fractal Organization* (Wiley, 2009)

It all starts with crafting a narrative so meaningful and moving that it induces belief-shifting epiphanies. Once the epiphany has occurred, the practice of behaviour change begins.

When crafting a narrative for a product, I immerse myself in its world, from the weeds of feature mechanics, to the helicopter view of market spaces, zooming all the way out to shifts in technology and culture. From this exploration, a storyline emerges that joins the dots to reveal the context − the positioning − of the product. This storyline determines the strategy for reaching and engaging people; it influences the place you hold in their hearts and minds and what you build next.

Narratives of disruption follow a similar pattern. Tying your disruptive mission into epic shifts that are creating pressure for change; vividly showing the painful consequences of failure to rise to your call to adventure; and drilling into the detail of how your mission addresses these issues − to create a better world in ways that no one else can because you have a unique combination of traits − is the stuff of disruption. A disruptor's role is to create a movement, not a mandate, by embracing their own weirdness.

Your life purpose may be a perpetual work in progress, but the endgame your quest is shooting for must be vivid and measurable so that you − and everyone who comes with you − grasps the current reality and what it'll take to realise the desired outcome.

When you've positioned your disruptive quest in this way – with boldness, with clarity of destination and a starkly contrasted picture of the old versus the new world – the work begins of weaving your vision, values and sense of meaning and purpose into everyday conversations with stakeholders and collaborators. Disruptors sprinkle magic meaning-dust all over everyday work so that even the most mundane task is no longer another to-do but a vital step on your journey towards a new and better world.

The third key: create feedback loops

Everyone and their dog talks about 'agility' these days, for good reason. As life becomes more complex and unpredictable, frequently checking that we're on the right track and adapting our plans on the fly is less risky than long-term roadmaps that assume we have all the answers up front, only to reveal that the thing we've spent ages working on misses the mark.

Agility is about a 'test-and-learn' approach, seeking feedback as early and often as possible to optimise what we're doing and stay on track.

Too often we're persuaded by experts to use cookie-cutter tactics, yet scaling tech companies has shown that a channel, tactic or message that works in one situation may not work in another.

Best principles trump best practices. Learning from others can inform our hypotheses, but the more knowledge and experience a disruptor amasses, the more aware they become of how little they know. 'Let's try it and see' is a winning mantra.

'The only true wisdom is knowing
you know nothing.'

– Socrates

One study of over 3,600 leaders found that the more experienced we are, the more we overrate our self-awareness. Although most of us believe we're self-aware, only 10–15% of people studied actually are.[65] These vital few are the disruptors, who intentionally disrupt their own mental models, often by seeking critical feedback from people who are willing to tell them the truth.

How much of what you think and say is heavily influenced by what you think others want to hear? Have you developed your own belief system, personal code and unique voice? Even this level of vertical development isn't sufficient to unleash our disruptive potential. We must advance to what psychologist Robert Kegan calls the 'self-transforming mind', at which point we can step back from our ideology and see it as limited or partial – we

---

65   Eurich, T, 'What Self-Awareness Really Is (and How to Cultivate It)', *Harvard Business Review* (4 January 2018), https://hbr.org/2018/01/what-self-awareness-really-is-and-how-to-cultivate-it, accessed 28 July 2022

become aware of how little we know.[66] We can hold more contradictions and opposites in our minds and no longer gravitate towards polarised thinking.

As we age, we pass through stages of development, making sense of the world around us. These stages are obvious in children, less so in adults. Advancement through these stages correlates with our ability to lead through times of change. Choose your experiments wisely, iterate quickly and 'only don't know'.

May the force of disruption be with you.

---

66   Kegan, R, and Laskow Lahey, L, *Immunity To Change* (Harvard Business Review Press, 1 January 2009)

Jane Young is originally from Shetland. She has held growth, innovation and leadership roles in agencies and tech companies, and has created visions and strategies for brands like 3M, Dixons and Hiscox to drive change, digitisation and collaboration.

Jane is a highly acclaimed speaker on the future of work, delivering keynotes around the world for the likes of Pfizer, Deloitte, Gartner, Cisco and WPP. Jane explores the future of work through the lens of growth, innovation and leadership and is currently immersed in scaling tech companies that help organisations transform working culture.

As founder of an agency that builds 'customer acquisition machines', Jane studies human behaviour, culture, storytelling and technology to help software as a service companies power growth through data, experimentation, creativity and bold thought leadership.

in www.linkedin.com/in/janesyoung

CHAPTER 16

To Thrive And Survive You Need A Media Company Mindset

MARK YOUNG

To be successful in this day and age, you must be ready to adopt a media company mindset. It doesn't matter if your company sells white sports socks or a complicated consulting service. In this digital age you *must* be seen online.

This is a lot easier than it was in the days of yore. Twenty years ago you would have needed actors, expensive camera equipment, scripts, lighting etc, or to hire an expensive media company that specialised in creating TV ads and videos. When you wanted to get your company's message out into the world, it was a costly endeavour.

These days, it is as simple as picking up your smartphone, pressing record and talking about what your customers want to know about your product or service. Having a media company mindset is vital. We live in a world now where people love to buy but they hate being sold to. How many times have you walked into a shop and been asked 'Can I help you?' And how many times have you responded 'No, I'm fine thanks, just looking'? It's because you want to see what is available by yourself first.

Most modern buyers will be 70% of the way through their buying process before they call or contact you. The buyer is acting with their own due diligence. They are checking to see if your product or service is going to solve their specific pains. They are checking in on your pricing, how you compare to competitors, what issues they may experience and what the reviews say about you.

The buyers will know far more about you than you will ever know about them. The 'zero moment of truth' is the first time you'll really know who the buyer is, because it's only after they've done the research that they'll give you a call or send an email to start a conversation. That's when you know the potential client exists – although they may have known about you for a while, because they have been researching you, reading blogs and watching videos.

What potential customers find online about you or your business today influences their purchasing choice.

An online presence

A business associate of mine once described social media as 'the emperor's new clothing', which could be here today and gone tomorrow. According to him, it was just a technique to squander time. He *hated* social media and still does, but let me tell you a story.

Once upon a time we were looking for a digital marketer and I had already found a few highly experienced candidates. I presented the potential CVs to my associate and asked for his feedback. He came back the next day and told me, 'No! I don't like those people. I don't think they are any good.'

I asked for his reasoning. It seemed strange to me that these highly skilled people were not even going to be considered. His reasoning was that he had looked over their social media profiles and decided that, because they didn't have many followers, they couldn't be good at their jobs. He thought that a skilled digital marketer / social media person would have built a larger following. For another individual there was no content. Why would we take on someone who wasn't creating content or developing their own personal brand, over someone who was fully focused on making sure they looked good online? It's like meeting an expert at a networking event and then sending them to an empty website.

It was amazing. My business associate, who had told me that social media was pointless, was now actually making purchasing decisions based on what he saw online.

If I were to Google you or your business what would I find online about you? You don't even have the choice about whether you are researched and found online. If people can't find you or there's not enough information to help them make their buying decision, they'll go somewhere where they can make a better-informed choice.

What exactly does it take?

Here are four things you need to do to have a media company mindset:

1. Create a culture of content and become the Wikipedia for your industry

What do you want to be recognised for? Are you producing interesting and educational content? Are you writing blogs? Producing videos? Do your social profiles and websites talk about who you help, how you help, and why the potential clients should care? I see too many social media profiles talking about themselves, about their own skillsets and not about how they help the potential client who is doing their research.

I am a firm believer in the business philosophy of They Ask, You Answer created by Marcus Sheridan, which states that the only content we ever need to produce is the answer to the questions our clients and potential clients ask. If the client asks a question, we are obliged to answer it. We must make it easy for the client to find the answer otherwise they will go elsewhere – probably a competitor's site.

You need to generate content around the questions your audience is asking. Remember, clients are doing their research and will not contact you until they are satisfied that you can help them with their needs. Your marketing teams and sales teams need to work together as revenue teams. It always surprises me how marketing and sales have distanced themselves from each other. Your sales team are generally the ones speaking with clients every day and hear all the questions that clients ask. This should be reported back to the marketing department for them to create the content.

2. Create videos

The demand for video content is rising and shows no signs of slowing down. HubSpot reported that the appetite for video content extends beyond entertainment purposes. Over half of customers want to see *more* video material from a company or business they follow on their social media sites, and the social networking sites like people who watch videos – but why?

Videos are prioritised over other types of content because watching a video on a social media site usually keeps you there for longer, and the longer you stay the more opportunity the site has to show you adverts or job posts, which is how the social sites make their money.

Video can significantly increase your credibility and raise your know, like and trust (KLT) factor, which makes people more likely to do business with you and refer you. A client told me that he was wandering around a trade exhibition when a complete stranger approached him and began conversing with him as if he were a long-lost friend. The stranger had been watching his content for a while so felt like he knew my client, even though the client didn't know him.

Video is excellent since written content can be created from it. You might take that video information, transcribe it into written format, and optimise it for social media before using it in a blog post or article.

Video is one of the simplest ways to capture an audience's attention and offers you a deeper connection with that audience. Research states that 69% of individuals would rather watch a video than read text to learn about products and services.[67] If you are the one in the video, then the viewer will be looking into your eyes. They can

---

67   Santora, J, 'Video Marketing Statistics: What You Must Know for 2022', Optinmonster (7 January 2022), https://optinmonster.com/video-marketing-statistics-what-you-must-know, accessed 26 July 2022

see you, they will hear you and they will know you. No clever words will build a connection with your audience as much as a video can.

A few more quick stats on why you need to be constantly creating video for your website, social channels and in your prospecting process:

- 85% of marketers credit video as an effective way to get attention online.

- 81% of marketers intend to use video marketing as part of their overall marketing strategy in upcoming years.

- 81% of marketers credit video with helping them to generate leads.

- People recall around 95% of the knowledge they learned from videos, as opposed to the information they may have read.

Video will not disappear, and you must embrace it as you adopt this media company mentality. It's not just about marketing. You should use video in your prospecting, during sales calls, after sales calls, and in customer service. The more you can humanise your brand, the more successful you will be.

3. Be consistent

You will not see any results from your content creation if you only produce one piece every month. You should be writing at least three blog articles per week, making eight videos per month for your website and posting at least once a day on each social media channel.

My preferred social channel is LinkedIn and I aim to post at least once a day to ensure that people are seeing me, but also because it is something that social media networks appreciate; when they notice your consistency, your content will be shown to more people. If you only publish once in a while then fewer people will be exposed to your content. Remember – people make purchasing decisions based on what they see online.

If you claim to be a forward-thinking company, but your Facebook page has not been updated in a year, then you will lose a little bit of credibility.

4. Promote and reuse your content

Top USA marketer Jay Baer once said, 'Content is the fire and social media is the gasoline.'[68] If you generate an excellent piece of content, you should consider how you will distribute it across all channels and whether you can convert it into different content types.

---

68   Baer, J, 'Why Content is Fire and Social Media is Gasoline',
Convince&Convert, www.convinceandconvert.com/content-marketing/why-content-is-fire-and-social-media-is-gasoline, accessed 26 July 2022

The next time a potential client asks you a question, be sure to answer it; but if it's an FAQ then make a video answering the question and put this onto your YouTube channel and website. Send the link to the client and then not only will they see the answer to their question visually, they'll also be exposed to all the other videos and questions they hadn't thought of yet and will gorge on that content, adding to your KLT.

You must hang out and deliver content on the channels where your clients hang out. You could be the best in the world at what you do but if you don't provide people with the opportunity to evaluate you then they will go elsewhere.

A conference speaker approached a friend of mine who ran a start-up training school. This speaker offered his services and they sounded pretty good, but when she Googled the individual she was unable to locate him.

She searched for him on LinkedIn and Facebook and couldn't find him. He was invisible to the world and she declined his offer. My friend made a purchasing decision based on her research (buyers' journey). She couldn't find anything about this individual to give her reason to carry on a conversation.

If you want to survive and thrive in this modern world, you must think like a media company.

Mark Young is a serial entrepreneur with a background in running companies in the technology, training and social media industries. He now runs the Modern Sales Academy and is an authorised coach for the They Ask, You Answer business philosophy that helps business owners, marketing and sales teams align to create shared growth goals and position their business as *the* trusted resource in their industry. At the core of They Ask, You Answer is a simple idea: educated prospects become happier, better customers.

Outside of work, Mark enjoys reading books around influence and persuasion and can be found inside the world of virtual reality. Anyone for a game of VR table tennis?

in www.linkedin.com/in/markyoungsocial

AFTERWORD

Disruptors may be everywhere, but they are certainly not in the majority. When the concept for this book was first proposed, I wasn't sure if the market would be ready for it. I've been in the book business for many years, and although I am a proponent of writing for a niche audience, sometimes you can be 'too niche'.

Luckily, I was surrounded by a group of experts much cleverer than me, and I was soon convinced that this book was exactly what was needed in these strange and challenging times. Over the past decade we have lived through several recessions, a global pandemic, and unprecedented division and fear. It is precisely those who are willing and able to disrupt the status quo who will take society to the next chapter in its evolution. It is the disruptors who have always led the way in times of positive change.

I hope you enjoyed reading the different perspectives on disruption, and I hope at least one or two chapters made you think about yourself and your contribution to society. If so, consider yourself a disruptor! There was quite a bit of discussion about whether the title of this book should be *Success Secrets of Disruptors* or *Success Secrets for Disruptors*. We eventually chose the first title, acknowledging the talent and wisdom of the authors while knowing that the book will resonate with people who are inspired to join us and step up.

Welcome to the world of disruption for positive change. We look forward to hearing about your exciting projects and supporting you in any way we can.

Mindy Gibbins-Klein
Award-Winning International Speaker, Author and Entrepreneur